Project Management Fundamentals

KEY CONCEPTS AND METHODOLOGY

Project Management Fundamentals

KEY CONCEPTS AND METHODOLOGY

Gregory T. Haugan

ﬀﬀ
MANAGEMENTCONCEPTS

ʄʄʄ
MANAGEMENTCONCEPTS
8230 Leesburg Pike, Suite 800
Vienna, Virginia 22182
Phone: (703) 790-9595
Fax: (703) 790-1371
www.managementconcepts.com

Printed in the United States of America

Library of Congress Cataloging-in-Publication Data

Haugan, Gregory T., 1931–
   Project management fundamentals : key concepts and
   methodology / Gregory T. Haugan.
      p. cm.
   Includes bibliographical references and index.
   ISBN 1-56726-171-X (pbk.)
      1. Project management. I. Title.

   HD69.P75H3774 2006
   658.4'04—dc22

                                                          2005054923

About the Author

Gregory T. Haugan, PhD, PMP, has been a vice president with GLH Incorporated for the past 20 years, specializing in project management consulting and training. He has more than 40 years of experience as a consultant and as a government and private sector official in the planning, scheduling, management, and operation of projects of all sizes, as well as in the development and implementation of project management and information systems.

Dr. Haugan is an expert in the application and implementation of project management systems. He participated in the early development of WBS and C/SCS (earned value) concepts at the Department of Defense and in the initial development of PERT cost software. He was the Martin Marietta representative on the Joint Army Navy NASA Committee developing the initial C/SCS concepts. He is particularly expert in the areas of scope management, cost management, schedule management, setting up new projects, and preparing proposals.

Dr. Haugan received his PhD from the American University, his MBA from St. Louis University, and his BSME from the Illinois Institute of Technology.

To my wife, Susan, for her love and support

Table of Contents

Figures

Preface

The collection and documentation of tools, techniques, and principles of project management followed similar work on scientific management in manufacturing by approximately 50 years. Efficient and effective management of projects required a unique system, just as the scientific management of the first decade of the 20th century was unique to manufacturing processes. The current practice of project management cuts across and integrates all the legacy systems within the enterprise and, using concepts from engineering, economics, accounting, and basic management, integrates and focuses them on delivering products, services, or results.

APPROACH

This book is designed to take the mystery out of the project management process for the new manager of a small- to medium-sized project. By "small-to-medium," we mean projects that have the following characteristics:

- Multiple projects per person or team

- Shared resources

- Frequent changes in project priorities

- Limited in-house resource base

- Working project manager

- Limited impact of project failure on the enterprise

- Matrix organization structure.

Although precise definitions of small or large projects are impossible, the concepts and basic management techniques, principles, and methodology are, at their core, independent of project size. This book takes a "back-to-basics" approach using conventional project management terminology that avoids inventing new terms for old concepts or alternate ways of packaging concepts to appear new or cutting edge.

The book contains a step-by-step methodology that is like a cookbook, except that it explains why each step is important and presents information on tools and techniques in the context of how they are applied. It also provides a refresher for experienced project managers to remind them of the essential discipline necessary to manage a project effectively without getting caught up in trying "magic bullet" solutions for common problems. It also can serve as a basis for the project manager of a larger project to make sure that all the basic principles and issues are addressed before introducing more sophisticated project management tools and techniques.

Project Management Fundamentals: Key Concepts and Methodology is also designed to be used as the basis for an internal methodology when tailored to a specific organization's unique requirements and way of doing business. In many cases, the guidance presented in the book may simply reinforce and add credibility to commonsense procedures already in practice in the enterprise. The reader can then comfortably adapt those procedures to his or her own project and organization.

This book is unique in its approach and content. In addition to presenting and discussing the accepted basic project management principles in the form of a detailed, step-by-step methodology, it also demonstrates how to apply that methodology to specific scenarios. The book does not assume that "one size fits all" regarding how to get a project started. While applying project management concepts, the book recognizes that at least seven different roles or scenarios determine how the project is actually managed and how the methodology should be implemented. These different approaches are derived from the following scenarios:

1. Direct internal assignment

2. Direct assignment (to support another organization)

3. Contract project manager (outsourcing)

4. Responding to a solicitation

5. Performing to a contract

6. Starting a life-cycle program

7. Taking over an ongoing project.

Each of these scenarios requires a different approach when starting the project, which affects the implementation of the methodology and the use of the project management tools. The reader should be able to identify his or her work situation in one of these scenarios and pick up important project management concepts and ideas.

ORGANIZATION AND CONTENT

The book focuses on the core methodological elements of project management and demonstrates how applying the methodology varies depending on the circumstances and organization, for example, whether you are a customer or a client.

This book is divided into four major parts:

- Part 1, *Introduction and Overview,* presents the basic principles and processes of project management and puts them in perspective.

- Part 2, *A Project Management Methodology,* presents a detailed discussion of each of the 10 major steps of the project management process and their substeps.

- Part 3, *Applying the Methodology,* identifies seven scenarios and discusses applying the methodology and principles to different types of situations

- Part 4, *Environmental and Facilitating Elements,* provides an introduction to and understanding of the other important aspects of project management that support the basic methodology.

The book concludes with five short appendices that present additional dimensions. Appendix A presents a discussion of project management maturity; Appendix B includes brief summaries of two advanced project management concepts: earned value management and critical chain; Appendix C addresses life cycles; Appendix D presents material related to the uniqueness of information technology projects; and Appendix E discusses the natures of several different types of projects.

A bibliography of references used in this book and additional recommended references is also included.

Gregory T. Haugan
Heathsville, Virginia

Acknowledgments

I received a great deal of assistance with this book, although all of the persons who helped may not be aware of it. The book's genesis was a short "primer" that Dr. Ginger Levin and I wrote when we were working together at GLH, Inc., in Falls Church, Virginia. The primer was used in our consulting business. Other input was provided by Dr. Lew Ireland, who also worked with us when we were using and applying the methodology of the primer with our clients. Jayne McQuade and Porter Kier of Northumberland Public Library helped me track down some of the reference materials, and Stewart Meny indirectly provided input as I watched him struggle to resolve master schedule and earned value management issues on the project he was working on as this book was being written.

I want to thank Jim Hayden of Capital One and the Central Virginia Chapter of the Project Management Institute (PMI®), who provided useful input on his current and past projects and how he manages them; I recognize how important it is to get input from project managers on the firing line. Special thanks go to the four reviewers of my drafts: Rick Peffer from the IRS in Tallahassee, Florida, whom I met at a PMI® function and who also provided some of the material for the figures and tables, the input for the information technology appendix, and good information on the use of PM on information technology projects in general; Jeff Carter of Rockwell Collins in Iowa, who also provided material and many recommendations for the book and has one of the best PM programs that I have had the pleasure to witness (he is also an instructor in PM at DeVry University); Arnold Hill, the project manager for a major government project, who took time from many more urgent activities to critique the drafts and provide insightful comments; and Lee Allain, a retired, experienced project manager who is deeply involved in county planning and conservation activities yet who took time to provide an important set of comments and perspective that improved the book considerably. In addition, Michael Dobson, an author of several project management books published by Management Concepts, provided very useful comments and insights. Thanks also to Reid Pierce Armstrong, who graciously provided the cover photo.

Finally, thanks have to go to the staff at Management Concepts for their great editing work and support over the past several months, especially Myra Strauss.

PART 1

Introduction and Overview

> ... it will be seen that the development of a science to replace rule of thumb is in most cases by no means a formidable undertaking, and that it can be accomplished by ordinary, every-day men without any elaborate scientific training; but that, on the other hand, the successful use of even the simplest improvement of this kind calls for records, a system and cooperation where in the past existed only individual effort.
>
> —Frederick Winslow Taylor,
> *The Principles of Scientific Management,* 1911

To F.W. Taylor, scientific management was a policy of establishing, after scientific study and research, a standard way of performing each industrial operation with the best possible expenditure of material, capital, and labor.[1] His principles—and those of Harrington Emerson, Henry Gantt, and others—revolutionized the manufacturing industry in the decade preceding World War I. These principles are followed today in manufacturing processes, and extensions of them provide the basis for today's project management body of knowledge. The concept of using a standard methodology to perform project management functions is the same concept used by F.W. Taylor in his philosophy of "one best way."

The recognition that managing projects required management skills and techniques different from those required for managing manufacturing processes arose in the late 1950s when the Cold War required that the United States develop large, complex weapons systems. Much of the learning effort up to this point involved developing principles to manage large companies, organizations, and production processes.

These new weapons systems development activities involved integrating the work of several companies involving many disciplines, not just civil or mechanical engineering, to develop one product. Most of the modern project management principles processes and practices evolved from the lessons learned in managing early weapons systems development.

These new weapons systems had five things in common: (1) they were one-time efforts and therefore temporary in the sense that the end products were not endlessly replicated, such as occurs on a production line; (2) they had a specified time by which they had to be completed; (3) they had a specified price or budget for the work to develop the end product; (4) the required performance of the final product was specified; and (5) they were complex and required coordinating and integrating the activities of several organizations and disciplines in every step of the development process.

Just as scientific management principles were documented in the period from 1910 to 1920, project management principles and practices were documented in many books and magazine articles starting in the 1960s. The project management body of knowledge was initially documented in 1996 by the Project Management Institute (PMI®) in its *Guide to the Project Management Body of Knowledge* (the *PMBOK® Guide*).[2]

KEY CONCEPTS OF PROJECT MANAGEMENT

An understanding and appreciation of the evolution of project management is useful when applying the techniques to individual problems and situations. It is important to understand why a step in the project management process is performed so that you can effectively tailor that step to individual projects and organizations.

Project management today, just like scientific management of Taylor's day, still involves records, a system, and cooperation, although these now are called data collection, planning and control, and communications.

The core of this book is the application of a basic project management process or methodology that consists of a number of steps performed in sequence, some of which usually require more than one iteration. Several of these steps, in turn, have subprocesses that also involve defined steps.

While all projects can be managed successfully by following these steps, the effort and emphasis placed on performing each step must be tailored to the specific project, the environment in which it is being implemented, and its origin. For example, every project requires planning, but the planning for a major aerospace project is far more extensive than that required for a two-week project involving two people developing a marketing brochure. Similarly, the planning that is performed when responding to a request for proposals (RFP) is different from that required for a new project assigned by a supervisor. In recognition of the importance of these differences, Part 3 of this book presents seven scenarios of different conditions or situations the project manager may encounter. Part 3 tailors the basic methodology presented in Part 2 to each of these scenarios.

DEFINITIONS

The world of project management is full of jargon and acronyms. Figure 1.1 presents a set of definitions of the most common project management terms used frequently in this book. These definitions are commonly used in the project management field and are included in similar form in the glossary of the *PMBOK® Guide*.[3]

More definitions will be added later as we build on this foundation. Once a project team member or leader becomes comfortable with the terminology, the principles and the process will not seem as daunting.

Figure 1.1. Key Project Management Terms

Program: (1) *A group of related projects managed in a corresponding way to achieve a broad common objective.* Programs could include such items as an antismoking program," a product marketing program, or an anti-terrorism program. Each of these programs contains several projects that are often being performed simultaneously. (2) *The collective related work that is performed by a series of projects as part of a program life cycle.* Programs may include an element of ongoing work until the life cycle of the program is completed. A typical U.S. Air Force aircraft program is an example. It starts with a concept to meet a need and proceeds through development, production, and operational service and retirement, all the time being managed through a program office.

Project: *A temporary endeavor undertaken to create a unique product, service, or result.* The emphasis is on the word "temporary," indicating there is a defined end date for the project and the word "unique," which implies something not done before.

Plan: *An intended future course of action.*

Project Schedule: *A graphical and/or textual representation of the planned time periods for performing project work activities and the planned dates for meeting milestones.* Schedules or related portions of schedules usually list the activities and milestones in chronological order. Schedules also may include actual start and completion dates for activities and actual completion dates for milestones.

Activity: *An element of work performed during the course of a project that normally has an expected duration, expected cost, expected level of quality, and expected resource requirements.* Activities have defined beginnings and endings. The terms "activity" and "task" are frequently used interchangeably, but "activity" is preferred and used in this book to differentiate from a "task" in a statement of work, which usually involves many activities.

Baseline: *An approved plan for an aspect of the project that is used as a basis for project control and project change control.* The term applies to schedules, cost estimates and budgets, specifications, drawings, and other items that define the product and performance.

Deliverable: *Any measurable, tangible, verifiable outcome, result, or item that must be produced, performed, or achieved to complete a project or part of a project.* The term is often used more narrowly in reference to an external deliverable, which is a deliverable that is subject to approval by the project sponsor or customer. A "deliverable" is sometimes referred to as an "end item," especially in government contracts. Also, a deliverable is sometimes referred to as a Contract Line Item Number (CLIN), especially in a government contract with are several defined deliverables. If it is a "service" project, the service provided is the deliverable, when completed; if it is a "results" project, the achieved result is the deliverable.

Stakeholder: *Any person or organization with an interest in the project.* Stakeholders include the sponsor, client, customer, project team, project manager, and user of the product.

THE PROJECT MANAGEMENT BODY OF KNOWLEDGE

The lead in monitoring and documenting project management practices transitioned from the public to the private sector in the 1980s with the major reductions in the National Aeronautics and Space Administration (NASA) space program, the end of the Cold War, and the rapid growth of the public sector's awareness of the importance of formal project management.

The Project Management Institute (PMI®), a professional association of over 100,000 members, provides a forum for the growth and development of project management practices through its conferences, chapter meetings, the monthly magazine *PM Network,* and its quarterly journal. In August 1987, PMI® published a landmark document titled *The Project Management Body of Knowledge,* which was followed in 1996 by *A Guide to the Project Management Body of Knowledge.* The *PMBOK® Guide* was updated in 2000 and again in 2004.[4] Two derivative documents focusing on the construction industry and on government also have been published. The *PMBOK® Guide* is intended to reflect the 40 years of experience gained in project management since the seminal work of the U.S. Department of Defense (DoD), NASA, other government organizations, and the aerospace industry in the 1960s.

The *PMBOK® Guide* documents proven traditional practices that are widely applied as well as innovative and advanced practices that have seen more limited use but are generally accepted. The material in this book is generally consistent with the material contained in the *PMBOK® Guide.*

THE BASIC PROJECT MANAGEMENT PROCESS

To understand the basic project management process, it is necessary first to discuss what is meant by "project management," and then how it is accomplished. Going back to Management 101 in college, "management" is generally defined as getting work done through people. The functions of management are planning, organizing, staffing, directing, and controlling (and, depending on the school, coordinating).

Project management can also be defined as the application of management functions, knowledge, skills, tools, and techniques to project activities in order to meet or exceed stakeholder needs and expectations from a project. In this definition, meeting or exceeding stakeholder needs and expectations invariably involves balancing competing demands among five items:

- Project goals and objectives: Where we are going?

- Statements of work (scope), time, cost, and performance: What do we have to do to get there, when, and for how much?

- Stakeholders with differing needs and expectations: Who is involved and interested?

- Identified requirements (needs and contract items) and unidentified requirements or expectations: What do the product, service, or results have to be able to do?

- Resource requirements versus availability: Which people are needed, and are they available?

The tools and techniques are embodied in the methodology presented in Part 2, and the knowledge comes from understanding the methodology and the explanations. The skills come from learning by applying the methodology to your particular situation.

Part 2 describes the application of a basic project management process and methodology to plan, organize, staff, direct, control, and coordinate a project. The methodology is applicable to projects of any size. It also can be used on parts of projects that are self-contained, down to the lowest level of the project—the activities. As we will discuss, the individual activities within a project require application of the same core project management principles as the overall project; the difference is in degree.

Figure 1.2 illustrates this basic project management process and methodology at the summary level.

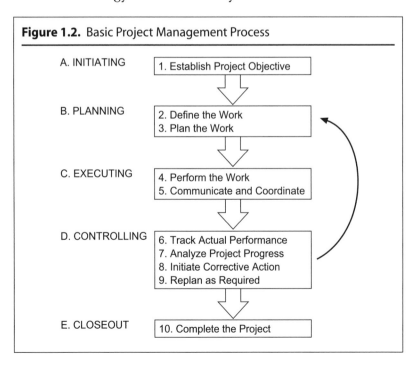

Figure 1.2. Basic Project Management Process

A. INITIATING — 1. Establish Project Objective

B. PLANNING — 2. Define the Work / 3. Plan the Work

C. EXECUTING — 4. Perform the Work / 5. Communicate and Coordinate

D. CONTROLLING — 6. Track Actual Performance / 7. Analyze Project Progress / 8. Initiate Corrective Action / 9. Replan as Required

E. CLOSEOUT — 10. Complete the Project

Each of the 10 major steps has a specific output that is defined, documented, explained, and discussed in Part 2. The steps are frequently iterative, that is, they may require revision and subsequent repetition. This constant iteration and replanning characterize day-to-day project management.

Because project management is a process with feedback loops, whenever the information system that collects the data for Step 6 and the analysis conducted during Step 7 indicate an adverse variance and a requirement for corrective action, the process is repeated for those portions of the project that are affected. This may involve one or more steps of the planning phase and perhaps even rethinking the goals and objectives established in the initiation phase.

Many years of project management experience have demonstrated again and again that following the basic project management process steps is essential to ensuring success. The process and methodology focus on achieving the project objectives within the classic project management triad of time–cost–performance, illustrated in Figure 1.3.

Figure 1.3. Project Management Triad

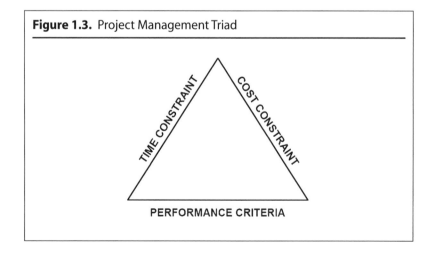

Working within these constraints is the constant challenge of project management:

• It is not possible to control costs if the schedule is slipping unless scope or product performance is changed.

• If the schedule slips, product performance is at risk if costs are held constant.

• If constantly yielding on one or more of the triple constraints of schedule, cost, and product performance (quality) is acceptable, there is no project management challenge or problem.

Many individuals do not manage projects well, and organizations do not always provide a supportive environment. Project management is a discipline and it requires discipline. It involves work. There are no magic panaceas available to enable the project manager to be successful without working at it. Following the proven methodology presented in this book will significantly reduce the possibility of a project's failure, which we define as having an unhappy customer because expectations regarding cost, schedule, or performance requirements were not met.

RELATED CONCEPTS

The project management process and methodology cannot be implemented in a vacuum. Certain related concepts provide a foundation and setting for the methodology:

1. *Basic management principles.* Project managers need to know more than what steps to follow to make the project a success; the job also requires working through other people, so the general principles of management cannot be ignored.

2. *Project environment.* The project is managed within a larger organizational entity; therefore, methods and tools for working in the specific enterprise environment and culture are important.

3. *Project Management Office (PMO).* The project manager needs an organizational framework for the project. As the project manager's workload increases, an efficient PMO significantly improves his or her ability to manage the project effectively and implement the required tools and methodology.

4. *Types of projects.* The project manager needs to be aware of the type of project being managed so that the right approach and tools are used.

5. *Life cycles.* Projects have life cycles, which are important to understanding and recognizing where each project is in the continuum.

These concepts are all discussed in depth in the following sections and appendices.

REFERENCES

1. Frederick M. Feiker. *How Scientific Management Is Applied* (Chicago: A.W. Shaw Company, 1911).
2. Project Management Institute. *A Guide to the Project Management Body of Knowledge (PMBOK® Guide)* (Newtown Square, PA: Project Management Institute, Inc.), February 1996.
3. Standards Committee. *A Guide to the Project Management Body of Knowledge (PMBOK® Guide),* 3d ed. (Newtown Square, PA: Project Management Institute, 2004).
4. Ibid.

PART 2

A Project Management Methodology

Management expert Peter Drucker discusses the need to analyze the work to be performed and break it down into steps: "As with every phenomenon of the objective universe, the first step toward understanding work is to analyze it. This, as Taylor realized a century ago, means identifying the basic operations, analyzing each of them, and arranging them in a logical, balanced, and rational sequence."[1] This is the fundamental concept behind Taylor's "one best way."

However, simply analyzing the work and identifying the steps is not enough; the steps must be integrated and put together into a process by individual members of a project team and the project team as a whole. Drucker, quoting Taylor, says: "We need principles of production which enable us to know how to put together individual operations into individual jobs, and individual jobs into 'production.'" Similarly, we need principles of project management to enable us to know how to put individual activities together into a final product.

Some of Taylor's fellow pioneers, especially Gantt, saw this clearly. The Gantt chart identifies the steps necessary to obtain a final work result. These are worked out by projecting backward, step by step, from the end result, identifying the activities, their timing, and their sequence. The Gantt chart was developed during World War I and was used effectively in industry and by General Crozier at the Frankfort Arsenal at that time. It remains the one tool we have to identify the process needed to accomplish a task, whether making a pair of shoes, landing a man on the moon, or producing an opera. Drucker believes that such recent innovations as the PERT chart, critical path analysis, and network analysis are elaborations and extensions of Gantt's work.[2]

But the Gantt chart is just one tool. It provides little information about many of the other elements that affect the project and about the other steps in the process.

Project work, precisely because it is a process rather than an individual operation, needs built-in controls. It needs feedback mechanisms that both sense unexpected deviations—and with them the need to change the process—and maintain the process at the level needed to obtain the desired results. The methodology discussed here is such an integrating device.

Figure 2.1 illustrates the basic project management stages:

A. Initiating

B. Planning

C. Executing

D. Controlling

E. Closeout.

As the project proceeds, it progresses through these five stages in turn—all of the stages are essential.

Except for the transition from the executing to the controlling stage, each stage is customarily characterized by a specific document being prepared and approved or a decision being made before proceeding to the next stage.

Figure 2.2 presents the stages and steps of the complete methodology, including the substeps. This part discusses

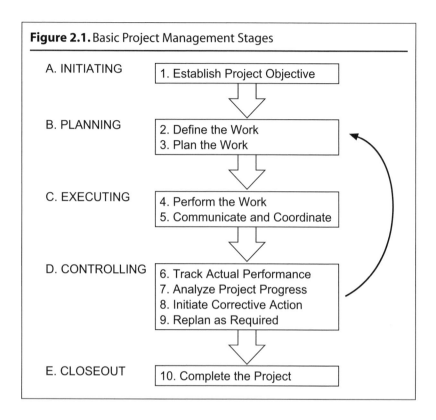

Figure 2.1. Basic Project Management Stages

each of these stages and steps in turn and explains their application. Part 3 relates them to specific project situations.

A. INITIATING STAGE

The initiating stage consists of those steps that must be performed before starting the detailed planning and performing the essential work of the project. The focus is on establishing and clarifying the project's goals and objectives and the ground rules under which the project manager will perform.

On large projects, the initiating or feasibility phase is planned and implemented as an independent project. The feasibility phase often uses sophisticated tools of economic

Figure 2.2. Stages and Steps of the Project Management Methodology

A. INITIATING	B. PLANNING	C. EXECUTING	D. CONTROLLING	E. CLOSEOUT
The work necessary to define objectives and constraints and get started	*Developing the detailed plans of the work to be performed*	*Doing the work to meet the objectives*	*Keeping the work on track to meet the objectives*	*Finishing in an orderly and satisfying manner*
Step 1. Establish Project Objectives 1.1 Develop statement of objectives 1.2 Define the deliverables and their requirements 1.3 Develop project (manager's) charter	**Step 2. Define the Work** 2.1 Develop the work breakdown structure 2.2 Prepare a statement of work 2.3 Prepare the specification **Step 3. Plan the Work** 3.1 Define activities and activity durations 3.2 Develop a logic network and schedule 3.3 Assign and schedule resources and costs 3.4 Develop the cost estimate 3.5 Establish checkpoints 3.6 Establish project baselines 3.7 Develop the project plan 3.8 Approve the project plan	**Step 4. Perform the Work** 4.1 Budget and authorize the work 4.2 Add staff resources 4.3 Produce results 4.4 Accommodate change requests **Step 5. Communicate and Coordinate the Work** 5.1 Coordinate the work 5.2 Prepare progress reports 5.3 Hold project reviews	**Step 6. Track Actual Performance** 6.1 Identify data and data sources/develop data collection systems 6.2 Collect and record the data **Step 7. Analyze Project Progress** 7.1 Determine variances 7.2 Perform analyses **Step 8. Initiate Corrective Action** 8.1 Identify action items 8.2 Facilitate the corrective action process 8.3 Arrive at a resolution **Step 9. Incorporate changes** 9.1 Change management 9.2 Perform routine replanning 9.3 Renegotiate scope (if necessary)	**Step 10. Complete the Project** 10.1 Prepare a closeout plan 10.2 Obtain customer agreement/notify team 10.3 Archive project data 10.4 Prepare "lessons learned" document 10.5 Send the customer the bill
Complete stage—move to Planning Stage	*Complete stage—move to Executing Stage*	*Complete stage—move to Control Stage steps*	*Complete stage—move to Closeout Stage*	*Complete project*

analysis, including parametric cost estimating, discounted cash flow analyses, cost-benefit analyses, and internal rate of return analysis, to determine the viability of the proposed project. For purposes of small and medium-sized projects, we will assume that the feasibility has been determined and that decision mechanisms and preliminary goals and objectives have been defined. The project is proceeding into the planning and implementation phases of the life cycle. (Of course, some of the work performed in the planning or start-up phase is dependent on the results of the feasibility determination or on requirements provided to the project manager.)

Step 1. Establish Project Objectives

1.1. Develop the statement of objectives.
1.2. Define the deliverables and their requirements.
1.3. Develop the project (manager's) charter.

After management reviews and approvals, which identify the end of the initial or feasibility phase, the project manager is selected or confirmed. The next level of detail of objectives or requirements is then determined. This level includes defining the project's duration, budget, and performance requirements. Key milestones also are established, the project organization and method of operation are determined, the project budget and resources are established, and deliverables or end products are identified.

1.1. Develop the Statement of Objectives
It is common to think of each project as having only one or more major objectives, but in fact, each phase, project, subproject, work package, and activity or task has an objective. These objectives relate to each other in a hierarchy founded on customer needs and requirements and the rationale and purpose for establishing the project. The objectives of

the project should be written down and discussed with the sponsor and the project team to avoid misunderstandings.

The Cheshire Cat in *Alice's Adventures in Wonderland* explains very clearly to Alice the reason for knowing your objective:[3]

> Alice: "Cheshire-Puss, would you tell me, please, which way I ought to go from here?"
> "That depends a good deal on where you want to get to," said the Cat.
> "I don't much care where—" said Alice.
> "Then it doesn't matter which way you go," said the Cat.
> "—as long as I get somewhere," Alice added as an explanation.
> "Oh, you're sure to do that," said the Cat, "if you only walk long enough."
> Alice felt that this could not be denied—.

The objectives of a project should be stated in terms of the same items that define a project: the product, service, or result to be delivered. They should be stated so that the project manager can readily determine if they have been met at the end of the project. Objectives go hand-in-hand with project requirements. In some organizations, the objectives are phrased as a vision or mission statement.

For purposes of this methodology, the objectives are stated in terms that address the overall scope of the project. Although they should be as specific as possible, they must be clear to the project team and the stakeholders. For example, the objectives of a project to develop a new Special Forces combat assault rifle could be to "Develop for the United States Special Operations Command the most reliable, rugged, accurate, safe, and ergonomic weapon available." This objective is very general and must be backed up by a specific set of product requirements that quantitatively define such items as the reliability, ruggedness, accuracy, safety, and ergonomic requirements.

Another objective might be to "Plan, manage, and implement an international global warming mitigation conference to be held in Seattle, Washington, in August 2007."

Or to "Perform a five-year study of the impact of acid rain on the forests of the Shenandoah Valley in Virginia."

Or to "Prepare a county comprehensive plan by the end of 2006 that meets state requirements."

Or to "Modify the company's tax preparation program to incorporate changes mandated by Congress in the Tax Reform Act of 2004. The changes are to be made in time to file the 2005 tax forms with the IRS."

The objectives may be either directed or negotiated and be described either in a contract or verbally, but they must be known and understood between the project manager and the sponsor or supervisor before the work can be defined. The objectives also need to be understood by all the participants and stakeholders so that decisions can be made in the appropriate context.

These principles serve as a checklist regarding the objectives of a project:

- Objectives are needed to establish the reasons for the project and to provide the framework for decision-making.

- The organization as a whole must contribute to accomplishing the objectives.

- Appropriate elements of the organization should contribute to the process of setting objectives.

- Organizational elements should be judged on their contributions toward meeting objectives.

- Project operational objectives or supporting requirements, such as time, cost, or performance, must be measurable.

These may be summarized as "SMART"[4]:

Specific
Measurable
Achievable
Realistic
Time-constrained

1.2. Define the Deliverables and Their Requirements

All the sample objectives are partially quantitative, but they do not tell the whole story. To be complete, they are complemented by quantitative "requirements," or the performance of the products that are to be delivered for which "what, when, where, how many, how much, and how good" are defined. It may not be possible to fully define all the requirements at the beginning of the project (depending on the type of project and the scenario). Nevertheless, it is important to start with as much definition as possible, recognizing that requirements might change and more detail will be developed as the project work is defined.

In some projects, requirements are stated in a combination of a contract and a specification, or they may arise from a directive from a supervisor or sponsor. These requirements will vary with the type of project and the scenario (see Part 3). In any event, the combination of quantitative performance criteria must cover the "what, when, where, how many, how much, and how good" of the project.

- *What* product is to be delivered, service is to be provided, or result is expected?

- *When* is the product, service, or result to be delivered or provided or the result completed?

- *Where* is the product delivered, the service performed, or the result to be provided?

- *How many* are to be delivered or provided?

- *How much* is the cost estimate or budget?

- *How good* does the product performance have to be, the service have to be, or how effective the result?

Two examples of quantitative project requirements are:

1. For an international conference the product would be the conference—the date is August 2007; the location is Seattle; the number of participants is 1500–2000; the number of speakers is 25; the budget is $1 million; and the overall success of the conference will be judged by the responses to a questionnaire provided to all the participants.

2. The county comprehensive plan is to be completed by the end of CY 2006—the state provides guidelines for the structure and content; five to 10 public hearings will be held; the budget is $100,000; and the quality or performance is judged by approval from the state and the county board of supervisors.

Products such as weapons, hardware, or systems purchased by the government have extensive requirements in terms of specific delivery items, dates and quantities, testing, and acceptance criteria. The specification describing performance of the products may be 200 or more pages, depending on the product, and often includes testing or inspection requirements. For a military rifle, even in a development project, the specification may include such details as trigger pull, weight, color, barrel materials, type of sights, ammunition to be accommodated, type of stock, and length. (More discussion of specifications is included in Step 2.3 of the methodology.)

In Step 1.2 of the methodology, depending on the scenario, the top-level performance requirements of the product and number of products should be known. However, the detailed requirements may await the more detailed definition of the planning stage or a preliminary design activity.

As the project manager, you need to know what you are to produce (or service to provide or results to achieve), when, and for how much. If you do not, you are just like Alice.

1.3. Develop the Project (Manager's) Charter

The project charter is a very important document to the project manager. It is the primary document used to define a project and to establish the general framework and organizational ground rules for the implementation phase.

The documentation of the objectives, requirements, and other elements in a project charter provides a mechanism to communicate and coordinate the purpose of the project to the stakeholders and to illustrate management support.

A corollary purpose of the charter is to make up for shortcomings in the level of project management maturity in the organization, as discussed in Appendix A, and the necessary support needed, as discussed in Part 4, Environmental Elements. The charter describes the required management support and the authority of the project manager and addresses the other important elements that normally would be in procedures and directives. This important step gives the project manager a mechanism to define the support required and to "negotiate" it with the appropriate managers in the organization.

A commonly used variant, the project manager's charter, serves as the "contract" between the project manager and the project sponsor or supervisor and establishes the parameters of the assignment, including resources and authority. It usually is prepared following an authorization to spend resources on a project and may include a statement of work.

The project manager prepares the charter, which then is reviewed and approved by senior management and, in some cases, the customer. In a matrix organization, it is important for the supporting organizations to concur as well. (See Part 4, Human Resource Management.) Project charters vary in size and comprehensiveness, depending on the size of the project. They usually are from three to 10 pages in length. (For small projects, the project charter may be a verbal agreement with the supervisor or sponsor; however, the project manager should document the agreement for future reference.)

One project manager for a new project in an organization that had no experience in project management or supporting project managers developed a charter in the form of a memorandum to the director. It contained his "understandings" of such items as space and facilities, hiring authority, personnel department and legal support, secretarial support, budget authority, and dates for the primary deliverables.

Paragraphs and sections within a project charter may vary from project to project and organization to organization, but Figure 2.3 shows the major areas addressed.

Figure 2.3. Generic Project Charter Outline

Project purpose
Project objectives and requirements
Summary project description
  • General description of the work
  • Description of the end product and expected quality or performance
  • Schedule and budget
  • Resources to be provided
Project manager
  • Responsibility
  • Authority
  • Coordination requirements
  • Reporting requirements
Facilities and environment
Supporting activities/organizations
  • Resources to be supplied
Customer and customer relations
Transfer or delivery of the end product

The outline must be tailored to the project's environment and culture. One relatively mature organization uses a "flexibility matrix" as part of its planning process, charter definition, and beginnings of discussion of risk. This simple presentation is illustrated in Figure 2.4.

Figure 2.4. Flexibility Matrix

	Least Flexible	Moderately Flexible	Most Flexible
Scope		X	
Schedule	X		
Resources			X

The charter should include all the information and guidance needed to start the project, add resources, and begin detailed project planning.

Figure 2.5 presents a sample project charter that is used in one organization both to define and to authorize work.

Figure 2.5. Sample Project Charter

State Department of Revenue
PROJECT CHARTER

Project Title: Property Tax Application System Mainframe Migration

Project Name:	Property Tax Application System Mainframe Migration	Date: January 10, 200X	
Agency:	ISP	Agency Contact:	Andy Wilson
Project Manager:	Andy Johnson		

APPROVER INFORMATION

Approver Name:	John Silversson	Role: Chief Information Officer/Director of ISP
Action:	Approve: X Reject:	
Approver Comments:	The project manager shall provide weekly oral progress reports.	
Approver Signature:	Date	

continues

Figure 2.5. Sample Project Charter (continued)

PROJECT DESCRIPTION

Project Background

The Property Tax Application System is run from the Unisys ClearPath mainframe system in ISP. Currently, plans call for the mainframe system to be decommissioned within the next few years. As a result, all systems currently processing on the mainframe must be migrated to other platforms.

Project Objective

The project is intended to document and evaluate the current Property Tax Application system and recommend a strategy to migrate from the mainframe to another platform. Recommendation must include current/future user requirements, suggested platform, tools, language, equipment needs, training needs, schedule, and scope of effort to develop a partial prototype. The recommendation report shall be completed within five months of approval of this charter.

Critical Success Factors

In-house resources must be used as much as practical. Current ISP staff must be able to support the current system and be trained to assume any developed system. No loss of user functionality is acceptable unless identified as unnecessary by Property Tax Administration management.

Constraints

Use in-house resources to every extent possible. Recommendation report must be available by June 1, 200X. Property Tax Administration personnel must be freed from project responsibility by June 1, 200X, in order to start the Annual Tax Roll process.

Resources

The project manager is assigned 50 percent of his or her time and will be supported by two ISP analysts at 100 percent of their availability runs out in June. Secretarial support will be provided as required by the CIO. Any funding requirements will be presented to the CIO for prior approval. Travel will also be authorized by the CIO on a case-by-case basis.

Project Authority

For the duration of this project, the two ISP personnel will report directly to the project manager. The project manager will provide appropriate input to the annual personnel reviews of the assigned persons. ISP department personnel shall be informed by memorandum from the CIO of the necessity and importance of providing full cooperation with the project manager, when requested. The CIO shall be informed of any conflicts so that appropriate priorities can be assigned.

Look at the project manager's charter as your contract with your organization regarding what, when, where, and how you are to do your job.

B. PLANNING STAGE

In their classic book on management, Koontz and O'Donnell write: "Planning is to a large extent the job of making things happen that would not otherwise occur."[5] They go on to state: "Planning is thus an intellectual process, the conscious determination of courses of action, the basing of decisions on purpose, facts, and considered estimates."

If there is a central project management principle, it is the primacy of planning. For many people, planning is the most difficult part of project management; nevertheless, without it a project manager cannot give direction to the team and there is no basis for controlling the project. This section presents the planning process step by step. When viewed this way, it is painless and in time becomes second nature.

Just as a contractor needs a set of plans to build a building, you as the project manager need a set of plans for your project.

Figure 2.6 provides an outline of this stage, which contains two major steps and eleven substeps.

Figure 2.6. Steps of the Planning Stage

---

2. Define the work
   2.1. Develop the WBS
   2.2. Prepare the statement of work (SOW)
   2.3. Prepare the specification
3. Plan the work
   3.1. Define activities and activity durations
   3.2. Develop a logic network and schedule
   3.3. Assign and schedule resources and costs
   3.4. Develop the cost estimate
   3.5. Establish checkpoints and performance measures
   3.6. Establish project baselines
   3.7. Develop a project plan
   3.8. Approve the project plan

Step 2. Define the Work

2.1 Develop the work breakdown structure.
2.2 Write the statement of work.
2.3 Prepare a product specification.

The second major step in the methodology is to determine the specific tasks or activities required to meet the objectives, that is, to determine the "scope." A combination of Steps 2.1 and 2.2 is sufficient to define the project's scope. Defining the work comprehensively provides a baseline for planning and control and assists in limiting "scope creep."

"Scope creep" is a virus that infects projects by adding work without corresponding resources or schedule or performance adjustments. It is caused by lack of configuration management and baselines.

The three tools used to define the work and provide the basis for defining the activities and the required resources are (1) the work breakdown structure (WBS), (2) the statement of work (SOW), and (3) the product specification. The product specification, as the name implies, is used on "product-type" projects. For the service and results categories, a "statement of objectives," as described earlier, will suffice. The product specification describes the required performance of the end items or deliverables.

2.1. Develop the Work Breakdown Structure[6]
The WBS is a device that assists the project manager in organizing and structuring the project work. It is based on a simple concept similar to an outline for a report or a book—only the sections are work elements and not chapters of a report or book.

Just like an outline for a novel or a report, the WBS represents an outline or logical decomposition of the work to be performed, focusing on the project's end item or deliverable. Developing a detailed WBS requires knowledge of how the product components will be assembled or integrated to form the final "product," the basic elements that comprise the "service" to be performed, or the methodology or steps to be taken to achieve the "result." This knowledge is required whether the final product is a report, an airplane, a building, an electronic system, a computer program, or any other output product.

It is important when preparing a WBS to focus on the output of the project, not the activities that are involved. One of the first important documents describing a WBS contains the following definition:

"A product-oriented family tree composed of hardware, software, services, data, and facilities. The family tree results from systems engineering efforts during the acquisition of a defense material item. A WBS displays and defines the product, or products, to be developed and/or produced. It relates the elements of work to be accomplished to each other and to the end product."[7]

The WBS should not be structured according to the functions performed or organizations involved—these are organization breakdown structures (OBS).

All WBSs have three types of Level 1 elements, as shown in Figure 2.7.

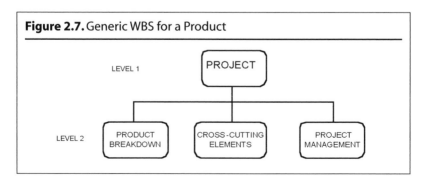

Figure 2.7. Generic WBS for a Product

The three types of elements are:

1. *Product (service or result) breakdown*—the physical structure of the output product being developed. For building a house, Level 1, or the product, would be "house." Level 2 could be roof, walls, foundation, and utilities. There may be more than one output product at Level 1. For example, an operator's manual may be an additional output or deliverable item with a product. (Instead of a "product," this may be a "service" or "result.")

2. *Cross-cutting elements*—a breakdown of items that cut across the product (Level 1), such as architectural design, final inspections of some products, or system test in others. These usually are technical in nature. There may be more than one element of this characteristic at Level 1.

3. *Project management*—a breakdown of the managerial responsibilities and activities of the project. This includes such items as reports, project reviews, and other activities of the project manager or his or her staff. (Conceptually, these are the project's "overhead.")

A WBS is decomposed to a level just above tasks or activities, sometimes referred to as the "work package" level. The product breakdown usually has several levels, while the cross-cutting or project management sections may have only two or three levels. Some parts of the product breakdown may require decomposition to a greater level than others because of the nature of the product and how it is to be put together. If an entire chapter of a report (or a major component of the house) is to be subcontracted, that may be the lowest level necessary if further decomposition is the responsibility of the contractor and the structure depends on the contractor WBS.

The work elements in a WBS are always nouns (floor, wall, wing, engine, motherboard, research, hazard analysis, etc.), and work packages also are identified by nouns. Verbs are used to describe tasks and activities.

A top-down decomposition of the work ensures that all the elements of the work are identified. An important rule is that each level represents 100 percent of the work that goes into the next-higher level of the structure. Subsequently, a bottom-up cost estimate can be developed by estimating the cost of performing the work described in each element of the WBS, starting at the activity level.

All projects need a structure for planning, but not all projects need a formal WBS. Except for the simplest projects, however, a WBS in the form of a written outline focusing on the end product is needed as a minimum. The WBS or the outline provides the basic framework to plan what work is to be performed.

Four sample WBSs are shown in Figures 2.8 and 2.9. The first two illustrate the process and one of the common formats. The third and fourth WBSs are presented in outline format. In the third example, the next level under each lowest-level element is where the activities would be identified. In the fourth example, Figure 2.9b, the WBS elements are shown in bold, and the Level 3 elements are activities.

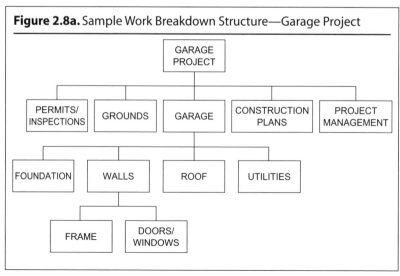

Figure 2.8a. Sample Work Breakdown Structure—Garage Project

Figure 2.8b. Sample Work Breakdown Structure—Software Project

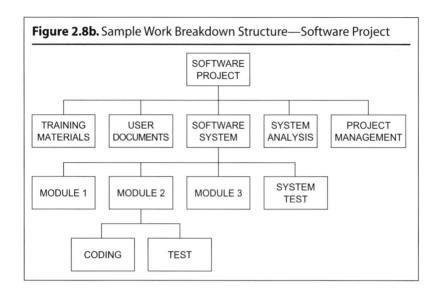

Figure 2.9a. Garage Work Breakdown Structure—Outline Format

1. Project management
   1.1. Financing
   1.2. Subcontracts
2. Construction plans
3. Permits and inspections
   3.1. Permits
   3.2. Inspections
4. Garage
   4.1. Foundation
   4.2. Walls
        4.2.1. Frame
        4.2.2. Drywall/paneling
        4.2.3. Doors/windows
        4.2.4. Assembly
   4.3. Roof
   4.4. Utilities
   4.5. Assembly
5. Grounds
   5.1. Driveway
   5.2. Landscaping

Figure 2.9b. IT Project Work Breakdown Structure and Activities—
Outline Format[8]

1.0. Business system alignment project
1.1. Project management
    1.1.1. Project start and completion
    1.1.2. Project planning
    1.1.3. Project reports
    1.1.4. Project administration
1.2. Business system alignment
    1.2.1. User registration and role mapping
    1.2.2. Process identification and mapping
    1.2.3. Database schema updates
    1.2.4. Business simulation testing
    1.2.5. Data cutover rehearsals
    1.2.6. Formal data cutover
1.3. Legacy data inventory and conversion
    1.3.1. Master data source identification
    1.3.2. Data conversion script definition and development
    1.3.3. Data conversion script execution
    1.3.4. Data conversion testing and validation
1.4. End-user training
    1.4.1. Training plan development
    1.4.2. Training material updates
    1.4.3. Training delivery
1.5. Postdeployment support
    1.5.1. WIP plan development and execution
    1.5.2. Postdeployment support
    1.5.3. Postdeployment training

When using a project management software package for
project planning, the outline WBS would be entered initially
with appropriate levels of indentation. The activities would
be identified under the appropriate element and indented,
making the WBS elements the summary levels and headings
in the outline of the project.

Work elements usually are given an identifying number,
known as the WBS number. Most common is the numbering
system shown in the outline version of the WBS in Figure 2.9,
but alphanumeric systems also are used in some projects.

A purpose of the WBS is to provide a framework for determining the activities to ensure that all the relevant project activities are identified. The activity definitions include information on who performs the work and when.

WBS Dictionary

A WBS dictionary is a document that defines and describes the work to be performed in each WBS element. It is used most often in medium and large projects and also when a standard WBS for a particular product has been developed. The information provided need not be lengthy, but it should be sufficiently descriptive that the reader understands what work is to be accomplished. Organizations at project management maturity Level 3 and above have sometimes found it useful to use a form to facilitate gathering WBS dictionary information. A typical form is presented in Figure 2.10.

Figure 2.10. Sample WBS Dictionary Form

Project Name _____Date: _____

WBS Number: _____WBS Name: _____

Parent WBS Number: _____Parent WBS Name: _____

Responsible Individual/Organization (if applicable)_____

Description of Work:

Child WBS Number: _____Child WBS Name: _____

Child WBS Number: _____Child WBS Name: _____

Child WBS Number: _____Child WBS Name: _____

Child WBS Number: _____Child WBS Name: _____

Prepared by: _____ Approved by:_____ Date:_____

Title:_____Title:_____

The data on the form are all that is needed for the minimum dictionary. In some organizations, however, more data are gathered, when applicable, such as budget, schedule, deliverables, and performance management data that may be part of a specific WBS element. Such data are useful for work packages but may not be applicable for summary, higher-level elements.

A typical WBS dictionary description for a WBS element named "training," which might occur at Level 2, is:

> *WBS 1.4. Training.* This element contains deliverable training services, manuals, accessories and training aids, and equipment used to facilitate instruction through which customer personnel will learn to operate and maintain the system with maximum efficiency. The element includes all effort associated with the design, development, and production of deliverable training equipment and instructor and student guides as defined in the list of deliverables, as well as the delivery of training services.

This description is almost suitable for a contract statement of work. In many cases, the WBS dictionary, with some rewording and some additions, becomes such a document.

One of the advantages of a WBS dictionary is the discipline of having to describe the work in each element in words. Frequently, the brief words describing a WBS element are vague or easily misunderstood, and the dictionary can dispel the miscommunication that might have resulted.

Some planners have found it useful to describe the WBS elements in terms of the activities performed in the element. This has the advantage of clarifying the work in the element without the need for a WBS dictionary. However, using activity nomenclature can be confusing and may tend to lose some of the discipline required for a nonproduct-based WBS. Another of the drawbacks of using activity-based WBS element descriptors is the difficulty of evaluating whether the 100 percent rule has been violated.

A WBS dictionary describing the work in each element can readily be converted into a comprehensive statement of work for a project or subproject, and the project manager can be confident that it addresses all the work to be performed. The total project scope is thereby clearly and comprehensively defined.

WBS Principles

These principles serve as a checklist when developing a WBS:

- The WBS should focus on project output—it is not an organizational chart.

- The sum of the elements at each level represents 100 percent of the work of the next higher level (the sum of the level 1 items is 100 percent of the project work or cost).

- The subdivisions should be logical and reflect the nature of the product, service, or result.

- The lowest level is the "work package" level, just above the activities.

- The lowest level should be sufficiently detailed to permit adequate control and visibility.

- The lowest level should not be so detailed that it creates an administrative burden.

- Each WBS element should have a unique identifier (e.g., a number).

- WBS descriptions for the work in each element may be developed and can be used for:

  – Work statements

– Work authorization

– Progress reporting

• The next level below the work package is the task or activity level. The same level need not exist for all activities.

• WBS descriptions should be nouns (activities include verbs).

• The WBS does not reflect time relationships or relations among activities.

• While a WBS element may have more than one activity at the next level, no activity can span two or more WBS elements.

Work Packages

A term and concept that is sometimes very confusing is the "work package." As noted, the lowest level of the WBS is referred to as the work package level.

The work package is defined as "the lowest-level work element in the work breakdown structure, which provides a logical basis for defining activities and assigning responsibility to a specific person or organization."

In Figure 2.9a, for example, each of the lowest elements in each part of the WBS is a work package. "Roof" and "foundation" at Level 3 are work packages, as is "utilities." Although these could be decomposed to the next level, these seem logical places to stop because each reflects a coherent package of work that logically would be assigned to one organization or skill.

A "roof" work package would include activities such as procuring or fabricating trusses; purchasing plywood, roofing paper, shingles, hurricane clips, and nails; and the labor involved in setting the trusses, laying the plywood, and laying the roofing paper and shingles. It would have an overall schedule for completion and an overall budget. If necessary or desired, the entire work package could be outsourced.

WBS in Project Management Software

For the purpose of clarifying principles and steps, we have been trying up to this point to "keep pure" when describing the WBS, work packages, and activity designation, but doing so can cause problems when using project management software.

Project management software has a column for the WBS number, but the software does not differentiate among true WBS elements, work packages, or activities. Therefore, every item on the schedule has a WBS number, including the activities and milestones. This has led to many persons thinking a WBS is a list of activities to be performed. The reason for consistency up to this point is that, conceptually, it is simply not correct to have an activity described as a WBS element, and developing a proper WBS is difficult if the elements include verbs, such as activities.

One of the software packages used to help develop a WBS, WBS Chart Pro™,[9] also uses this terminology. This package integrates seamlessly with Microsoft Project®, and a WBS generated using WBS Chart Pro™ can easily be transferred to MS Project®.

In summary, the WBS is used as the primary tool to define the project work. This is a multistep process, as shown in Figure 2.11.

Figure 2.11. Steps to Develop a WBS

Step 1. Identify the project objectives; this will assist in Steps 2 and 3.

Step 2. Determine the general type of project by identifying specifically whether the primary output is a product, service, or result.

Step 3A. If the project output is a product, Level 2 will include the product name, secondary product names, and cross-cutting elements. Make sure all project outputs can be related to a Level 2 element. (Proceed to Step 4.)

Step 3B. If the project output is a service, Level 2 will include the top-level groupings of the various types of work and the project management element. Consider identifying as many activities as possible and grouping them by logical categories related to areas of work (bottom-up synthesis). (Proceed to Step 5.)

Step 3.C. If the project output is a result, Level 2 will consist of the major steps in the acknowledged process necessary to achieve the result plus the project management element. (Proceed to Step 6.)

Step 4. For product WBSs, subdivide the product element into the logical physical breakdown of the product. Subdivide the cross-cutting elements into the supporting work. (Proceed to Step 7.)

Step 5. For service WBSs, subdivide the Level 2 WBS elements into logical functional work areas. (Proceed to Step 7.)

Step 6. For results WBSs, subdivide each Level 2 WBS elements into the standard processes specified to achieve the objective or output of the element. (Proceed to Step 7.)

Step 7. Review the work at each level to make sure 100 percent of the work is identified, adding elements as necessary. In a product WBS, make sure integrative elements are added as necessary.

Step 8. Continue to subdivide the elements to the work package level. Further subdivision would violate the principles outlined above. Stop when the next level would be activities or is unknown until further analysis or planning is performed. At the bottom level the complexity and dollar value of the elements become manageable units for planning and control purposes.

Step 9. Review the WBS with stakeholders and adjust as necessary to make sure all the project work is covered.

2.2. Prepare a Statement of Work

As stated previously, the goal of this book is to introduce the reader to project management principles and a methodology that will help their organization achieve at least Level 2 project management maturity. We would be remiss, therefore, if we did not include a more complete discussion of statements of work. This section therefore presents a description of some common broad interpretations of the statement of work and then covers its preparation as the required Step 2.2 of the methodology.

Broad Concepts of the Statement of Work

Both Cole[10] and Martin[11] have much broader concepts of the statement of work than are used in this book. Martin recommends a standard baseline SOW be used that includes the sections illustrated in Figure 2.12.

Figure 2.12. Standard Baseline SOW Framework[12]

- Table of contents
- Statement of confidentiality
- Introduction
- Services (or products) provided
- Roles and responsibilities
- Management procedures
- Hours of operation
- Facilities/tools/equipment requirements
- Schedule
- Pricing
- Signature block
- Glossary of terms
- Attachments

This SOW framework would be used when outsourcing, which is further discussed in Part 3, Scenarios 3 and 4 of this book.

Martin includes in his introduction sections titled "Purpose" and "Description of Work," which correspond to the objectives discussed in the methodology in Step 1 and the SOW discussed in this section. His "Services (or Products) Provided" describes the deliverables.[13]

Cole approaches the SOW from the perspective of a U.S. government document and presents another standard outline for an SOW in terms of the information it will contain. Figure 2.13 illustrates this approach.

Figure 2.13. Standard Outline for an SOW[14]

Part I: General Information
  A. Introduction
  B. Background
  C. Scope
  D. Applicable Documents
Part II: Work Requirements
  A. Technical Requirements
  B. Deliverables
Part III: Supporting Information
  A. Security
  B. Place of Performance
  C. Period of Performance
  D. Special Considerations

Cole includes in Part II the equivalent sections to our narrow definition of the SOW and the deliverables, and he includes the description of the project's purpose or objectives under the "Part 1, C. Scope" heading.

The U.S. Department of Defense also has a standard format for statements of work, which is presented in Figure 2.14.

Figure 2.14. MIL-HDBK-245D Statement of Work Format[15]

---

1. *Scope:* Include a statement about what this SOW covers. Some background information may be helpful to clarify the needs of the procurement.
  1.1. *Background* (Do not discuss work tasks in Section 1)

2. *Applicable Documents.* All documents invoked in the requirements section of the SOW must be listed in this section by document number and title.
  2.1. *Department of Defense specifications*
  2.2. *Department of Defense standards*
  2.3. *Other government documents*
  2.4. *Industry documents*

3. *Requirements:* The arrangement of technical activities and subactivities within the *Requirements* section will be dictated by program requirements. If a WBS is being used in the program, activities should be arranged in accordance with that WBS. It may be helpful to have a general activity to orient the planning and use of the subsequent subactivities.

The "1. *Scope*" section corresponds approximately to the Step 1 Objectives, and "3. *Requirements*" corresponds to Step 2.2 in this methodology.

In Step 2.2, the focus is only on the narrow description of the work defined within the WBS structure, recognizing that the term means much more to some organizations than to others.

According to DoD, the SOW is the document that "describes in clear understandable terms what project work is to be accomplished, what products are to be delivered, and/or what services are to be performed."[16] Preparing an effective SOW requires a thorough understanding of the products and services or results needed to satisfy a particular requirement or to meet a specific objective.

Because the WBS is based on what work is to be performed to deliver the end items, is used for the outline of the SOW, and the WBS dictionary, with minor modifications, can readily be converted into SOW language. When the project is a component of a larger program, the WBS addressing the work to be outsourced is referred to as the contract work breakdown structure, or CWBS.

We will demonstrate later how the WBS is used as the basis for developing the cost estimate. An SOW structured according to the WBS ensures that all the work is described and makes this part of the project management planning much simpler.

An SOW expressed in explicit terms will facilitate effective communications during the planning phase and effective project evaluation during the implementation phase, when the SOW becomes the standard for measuring project performance.

Use of the WBS also will facilitate a logical arrangement of the SOW elements. You should provide a convenient checklist to ensure all necessary elements of the project are addressed.

Some SOW do's and don'ts, which can be found in the MIL-HDBK-245D, include the following:

DO:

- Work with a competent team and an experienced team leader.

- Exclude "how-to" requirements.

- Use the program WBS to outline the required work effort.

- Exclude design control or hardware performance parameters, because these should be covered in the specifications.

DON'T:

- Order data requirements in the SOW (use a separate data requirements list).

- Establish a delivery schedule in the SOW itself (may include major milestones for clarity).

- Invoke in-house management instructions.

- Use the SOW to establish or amend a specification.[17]

In general, use the SOW to simply describe the work. For this methodology, keep it simple.

In this step we add another dimension to the WBS by describing the work to be performed for each of its elements. This discipline requires us to think out each aspect of the WBS and therefore the project. This is planning!

2.3. Prepare the Specification
The specification preparation step applies primarily when the project output is a product and less frequently for a "service" or "result" project. Developing a specification for the output from a service or result project should be done whenever possible. For a result-type project, the specification would describe what performance the end result should achieve. The product specification is the document that describes the planned, desired, or required performance of the end items as well as the metrics or tests used to verify that the performance has been achieved. This document provides the baseline against which actual performance of the end item is to be measured.

The SOW should define the work to be accomplished on the project, as discussed in Step 2.2. A specification should contain a description of qualitative and quantitative design and performance of products. The SOW includes a reference to the specification, but it should not spell out the specific qualitative or quantitative technical requirements. For example, the referenced specification may cite reliability and maintainability requirements in terms of quantifiable mean-time-between-failures (MTBF) and mean-time-to-repair (MTTR); the SOW should simply state that the work is to establish, implement, and manage a reliability and maintainability program.[18]

The two general categories of specifications are detail and performance.[19]

- A *performance specification* states requirements in terms of the required results with criteria for verifying compliance, but without stating the methods for achieving the required results. A performance specification defines the functional requirements for the item, the environment in which it must operate, and interface and interchangeability characteristics.

- A *detail specification* specifies design requirements, such as materials to be used, how a requirement is to be achieved, or how an item is to be fabricated or construction. A specification that contains both performance and detailed requirements is still considered a detail specification.

Step 3. Plan the Work

3.1. Define activities and activity durations.
3.2. Develop a logic network and schedule.
3.3. Assign and schedule resources and costs.
3.4. Develop the cost estimate.
3.5. Establish checkpoints and performance measures.
3.6. Establish project baselines.
3.7. Develop the project plan.
3.8. Approve the project plan.

In this key third major step, the activities and resources required to achieve the specified performance and meet the project requirements are identified and a timeline established, costs are estimated, and a project plan is prepared and approved. The project plan documents the end of the planning phase and provides the basis execution, which is the next phase: Executing.

Although the substeps within Step 3 are discussed in series, experience shows that the first three are often accomplished in parallel or simultaneously when using project management software.

3.1. Define Activities and Activity Durations

Once the WBS is completed, the activities can be defined and their durations estimated. Since activities are the basic building blocks of the project—its DNA—they are most important to project management. One of the primary purposes of the WBS is to assist in defining the activities in an organized manner so that all the important activities are identified.

Developing the WBS as the basis for identifying necessary activities provides an effective methodology for those who otherwise have trouble planning.

3.1.1. Activity Definition

One of the key steps in project management is identifying the activities: the key building blocks for the project schedules, budgets, and performance. This section illustrates how to identify activities and describes their characteristics. Some may think that this project management concept is relatively recent; however, in 1911 Fredrick W. Taylor wrote the following about his principles of scientific management and the definition of activities (tasks in his terminology):[20]

In developing these laws, accurate, carefully planned and executed experiments, extending through a term of years, have been made, similar in a general way to the experiments upon various other elements which have been referred to in this paper.

Perhaps the most important law belonging to this class, in its relation to scientific management, is the effect which the task idea has upon the efficiency of the workman. This, in fact, has become such an important element of the mechanism of scientific management, that by a great number of people scientific management has come to be known as "task management."

There is absolutely nothing new in the task idea. Each one of us will remember that in his own case this idea was applied with good results in his schoolboy days. No efficient teacher would think of giving a class of students an indefinite lesson to learn. Each day a definite, clear-cut task is set by the teacher before each scholar, stating that he must learn just so much of the subject; and it is only by this means that proper, systematic progress can be made by the students. The average boy would go very slowly if instead of being given a task, he were told to do as much as he could. All of us are grown-up children, and it is equally true that the average workman will work with the greatest satisfaction, both to himself and to his employer, when he is given each day a definite task which he is to perform in a given time, and which constitutes a proper day's work for a good workman. This furnishes the workman with a clear-cut standard, by which he can throughout the day measure his own progress, and the accomplishment of which affords him the greatest satisfaction.

This description of the concept contains several characteristics of activities that are directly relevant to project management and this methodology.

"Tasks" (or activities) are characterized as belonging to a single person or organization, lasting for an estimated period of time, and having a related cost or budget. Although infrequently specified explicitly, activities also have performance or quality requirements, just like a project. If the activity is vague, it needs to be redefined. Figure 2.15 presents a list of activity characteristics.

Figure 2.15. Characteristics of Activities

- Work is performed and described in terms of a verb, adjective, and noun—that is, there is action performed.
- A single person or organization is responsible for the work. More than one resource may be assigned to an activity, but one person is in charge of delivering the output. If this is not the case, the item needs further decomposition or to have joint responsibilities clarified.
- It has a defined start point. There is a specific action that can be identified that marks the start of an activity or a predecessor activity that must be completed.
- There usually is a tangible output or product at completion. Projects normally also have level-of-effort activities or support activities without clearly defined outputs; the primary activities, however, have defined and measurable outputs. The point at which an activity is completed is determined by the availability of an output product that is used as input by a successor activity.
- It fits logically under an existing WBS element. If it does not, then either the activity is not part of the project and the WBS needs modification, or the activity is ambiguous and needs redefinition.
- It is of a size and duration that is sufficient for control. Activities that are too long do not provide sufficient time for corrective action if problems arise, and too many activities that are too short can make the cost of the control more expensive than a problem that may arise. However, using a rolling-wave concept in which the near-term activities are relatively short and those many months in the future are longer can make sense.
- Actual schedule status data can be collected for the activity. For schedule control, the start and end points must be sufficiently defined so that the start and finish of the activity can be reported.
- Actual cost (person-hour) data can be collected for the activity or work package that contains the activity. For cost or resource control, actual cost data or the actual expenditure of resources can be collected. Obviously, if tracking actual expenditures is not required, this principle can be ignored.
- The labor and costs necessary to perform the activity can be estimated. The resource requirements must be able to be determined in the planning phase.
- The activity represents a significant effort in support of project objectives. Trivial or incidental activities need not be included.
- Zero duration activities are milestones or events and represent the start or completion of another activity or set of activities. They should be included at the start and finish of the project to identify completion of key activities or groups of activities.
- *The activity may not be performed if it is not in the schedule or plan.* It is important to be able to communicate the need for an activity to the responsible person or organization. Charting it on the schedule or in the project plan is a method of identifying the work required.

If the lowest-level element of a WBS for a house project is the heating, ventilating, and air conditioning system (HVAC) work package, the activities at the next level could be:

1. Design the HVAC

2. Procure the HVAC components

3. Install the HVAC

4. Test the HVAC

5. Inspect and accept the HVAC.

(Note that each of the activities has a verb and a noun and meets the criteria. Also, the HVAC system is a work package.)

As another example, for the work package "landscaping," the activities to be performed could be:

1. Prepare landscaping layout

2. Order bushes, trees, and mulch

3. Regrade around the garage

4. Dig holes for plants

5. Deliver bushes, trees, and mulch

6. Plant bushes and trees

7. Plant grass.

Each activity has a specified and expected duration, resources, cost, performance, and output.

The duration of many activities depends on the quantity and quality of labor resources assigned to the activity. (Exceptions are physical phenomena such as "paint drying" and "concrete setting.") There is a minimum duration for an activity, however, no matter how many labor resources are assigned. There also is a maximum reasonable duration for each activity. This is the duration beyond which costs begin to increase significantly because of inefficiencies.

To estimate activity duration, historical data, previous project experience, expert judgment, supplier estimates, pooled experience from team members, and any other logical basis may be used. Schedules may be dictated by customers or sponsors and resources then assigned as necessary to meet the schedule requirements. (See Scenario 4 in Part 3.)

A "level of effort" is an activity that serves the function of a placeholder, providing a place to identify certain types of costs that are project-related but can be classified as "overhead." Typically, the costs or labor (e.g., the project manager and members of the project office) fit this category, as do various staff activities. The typical level-of-effort activity may be many time units long and may extend from the start to the end of the project, as in the example of a project manager, a secretary, and a staff assistant all assigning 100 percent of their time to the activity. These activities are identified in the project so that all costs involved in the project can be accurately projected.

Often, schedules are developed using a "master schedule," or an overall schedule for a deliverable that is established by a customer or sponsor. The durations of work packages or groups of work packages are then estimated and scheduled to fit within the overall requirements. The organizations responsible for the work packages then identify the activities and the resources required to complete the overall work package in the specified time period.

Activity definition involves identifying and documenting the specific activities that must be performed to produce the deliverables and to perform the work represented in the work packages. A WBS is decomposed to the "work package" level. Below the work package level are the activities where the work is actually performed and network planning is accomplished.

Figure 2.16 illustrates the relationship among the WBS, work packages, and activities for Project X, a new personal computer development project.

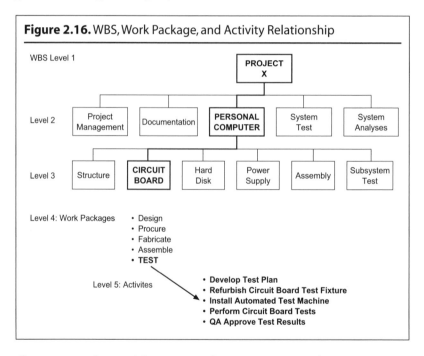

Figure 2.16. WBS, Work Package, and Activity Relationship

Cost-control considerations also come into play. Cost control is sometimes impractical at the activity level because of the difficulty in collecting actual cost data. However, where cost controls are applied, if the data cannot be collected at the activity level then they must be collected at the level above the work package level. Person-hour data also should be collected at the work package level but, depending on the project, may be collected at the activity level.

The "control account" is the term used to describe the management control element, such as the work package, at which actual cost can be accumulated and compared to budgeted costs for work performed. This is a key concept in a larger, advanced concept called "earned value," summarized in Appendix B.

In addition to ensuring that the entire scope of the project is addressed, the primary function of the WBS is to identify and define the activities that need to be performed in the project. The WBS provides the outline structure for Gantt charts and network planning and also outlines what work will be performed; the outlined activities describe the actions necessary to perform that work. This is illustrated in Figures 2.17 and 2.18 for a hypothetical automated ordering system. In Figure 2.17, note that the WBS elements are in adjective/noun form.

Figure 2.17. Example of WBS Elements

Automated Ordering System (AOS) Project

1.0. Project Management
    1.1. Project Start and Complete
    1.2. Project Meetings
    1.3. Project Reports
2.0. AOS Requirements Specification
    2.1. Initial AOS Requirements Specification
    2.2. Final AOS Requirements Specification
3.0. AOS Design Specification
    3.1. Initial AOS Design Specification
    3.2. Final AOS Design Specification
4.0. AOS Software
    4.1. AOS Module 1
    4.2. AOS Module 2
    4.3. Integrate Modules

In Figure 2.18, the WBS elements are in bold. The activities are in italics in verb/adjective/noun form at the level below the WBS.

Figure 2.18. Example of WBS Elements and Activities

Automated Ordering System (AOS) Project

5.0. Project Management
    5.1. Project Start and Complete
        5.1.1. Go Ahead
        5.1.2. Complete Project
    5.2. Project Meetings
        5.2.1. Prepare for Kickoff Meeting
        5.2.2. Start Kickoff Meeting
    5.3. Project Reports
        5.3.1. Prepare Interim Progress Report
        5.3.2. Deliver Interim Progress Report
6.0. AOS Requirements Specification
    6.1. Initial AOS Requirements Specification
        6.1.1. Create Initial AOS Requirements Specification
        6.1.2. Review Initial AOS Requirements Specification
        6.1.3. Update Initial AOS Requirements Specification
    6.2. Final AOS Requirements Specification
        6.2.1. Review Final AOS Requirements Specification
        6.2.2. Approve Final AOS Requirements Specification
7.0. AOS Design Specification
    7.1. Initial AOS Design Specification
        7.1.1. Create Initial AOS Design Specification
        7.1.2. Review Initial AOS Design Specification
        7.1.3. Update Initial AOS Design Specification
    7.2. Final AOS Design Specification
        7.2.1. Review Final AOS Design Specification
        7.2.2. Approve Final AOS Design Specification
8.0. AOS Software
    8.1. AOS Module 1
        8.1.1. Code AOS Module 1
        8.1.2. Unit Test AOS Module 1
    8.2. AOS Module 2
        8.2.1. Code AOS Module 2
        8.2.2. Unit Test AOS Module 2
    8.3. Integrate Modules
        8.3.1. System Test Integrated Modules
        8.3.2. Complete AOS Software

This example illustrates the relationship of the WBS to the activities. In the next step, we discuss how the individual activities are linked in the project management software into a precedence network. This is displayed in Gantt format on the screen and on hard copy.

The manner in which the WBS is arrayed can make schedules easier to read and use. Put the project management element at the top of the WBS and number it 1.0. If there is any natural process flow at Level 2 of the WBS, such as occurs often in "results" projects, have it flow from left to right in the graphic version of the WBS or top to bottom in the outline version, so that the schedules will be presented more naturally in the customary waterfall display.

A useful device to assist in scheduling is to establish a special work package under project management for the start and completion events of the project. Included in that work package are the two zero-duration activities or milestones that identify the start and completion of the project.

When the WBS data are entered into the project management software, it is a swift process to identify all the activities in the project and to arrange them in a logical schedule format. For each work package or lowest level of the WBS, ask how the work in the WBS element should be accomplished. Ask an expert if you do not know or are uncertain. If you and your teammates cannot define the activities, then perhaps you are the wrong ones to perform the work package or project.

Experience has shown that clearly defining activities or tasks is not as easy as it looks. Too many times they are inadequately defined, and poor schedules and communication problems result. Activity definition is extremely important because activities are the building blocks for planning and controlling the project.

The WBS elements 6.0 and 7.0 of Figure 2.18, the AOS requirements specification and the AOS design specification, are well-defined documents, and the activities involved are all clear. The outputs are tangible—something is done to the document. The activities of coding the software are similarly clearly defined. The output would be completed software code, probably hard copy as well as digital form, depending on the normal practices of the organization. Unit test is usually defined with the completion of a document provided by the quality-control organization or someone providing a similar independent function.

3.1.2. Activity Durations

The time durations should be estimated as the activities are being defined. In this section we discuss the different philosophies and methods of determining activity duration.

Estimating activity duration involves assessing the number of work periods (amount of time) needed to complete each identified activity. The person or group on the project team who is most familiar with the nature of a specific activity should make or at least approve the duration estimate.

Historical data, expert judgment, experience, and analogous estimating processes may be used to estimate duration. Information may be available from project files or commercial databases, but most often it comes from the knowledge of project team members. Constraints and assumptions should be considered. Sometimes, activity durations are set in advance or fixed, and the estimating involves determining the resources necessary to complete the activity within the set time.

Elapsed Time versus Work Time—Activity duration can be stated in minutes, hours, days, weeks, months, or any other time unit. If using software to assist in planning and scheduling, it often is possible to intermix the units and the computer will automatically adjust to an established default time period. Project duration would be the length of time to complete the entire project or to deliver the primary end item and close out the project.

In the feasibility and planning phases of the life cycle, it is customary to express activity durations in terms of "elapsed time" or "calendar time" in a Gantt format. These activity durations would include weekends, holidays, vacations, plant shutdown periods, and the like. Customers usually will express project durations in elapsed time, and these units are used in contracts and requests for proposals when specific dates are not feasible. For example, it is common to see that the delivery of an end item is stated as so many days or weeks after the award of the contract (DAC) or a Notice to Proceed (NTP). In all cases, these are elapsed time or calendar time and include weekends and holidays.

Certain types of activities also are always expressed in elapsed time. Common examples are concrete setting or paint drying. Also, when renting facilities or equipment, the duration is expressed in elapsed time.

However, it is normal to use working time when estimating the duration of individual activities. This is essential when performing bottom-up cost estimating, which is based on adding up the costs of individual activities to determine total project cost. The reason to use working time is that estimating is done in time units such as hours, and the cost is determined by applying a labor rate to the time units. Weekends and holidays are not normally working time.

When preparing the schedule in Gantt format or assigning specific calendar dates, nonworking periods must be considered. The specific dates depend on the calendar and whether or not there is a holiday in the planned time period. Project management software contains a calendar that defines which days are nonwork days and holidays and will automatically account for these.

Effort-Driven Activity Duration versus Fixed-Duration Activities—There are three different approaches to determining the duration of activities: (1) effort-driven, which is based on the amount of work involved; (2) fixed duration, in which the time span is predetermined; and (3) the PERT-time estimating algorithm. A combination of the first two is often used on the same project.

Effort-Driven Activity Duration—Effort-based activity durations require two data elements: (1) the estimated effort in terms such as person-hours or person-days and (2) the number of persons assigned to the activity. If the estimate is 80 person-hours for an activity and two persons are assigned, the activity duration is 40 hours, five days, or one work week. If only one person is assigned, the activity will take 80 hours, 10 days, or two work weeks.

The availability of resources influences activity duration and therefore the schedule. For example, a key person on vacation or a trip in support of another project could have a negative impact on the schedule.

Fixed-Duration Activities—Fixed-duration activities differ from the effort-driven activity duration model in that their duration is set first, and then the resources are assigned to complete the activity in the predetermined time.

There are three variations of the fixed-duration activity model:

1. Time-Critical Activities. For activities in which fixed durations are critical to meeting project delivery requirements, the resources are assigned to perform the required activity in the established time period. Multiple quantities of the resource may be required to complete it in the assigned time. For example, three engineers may be required to complete an engineering activity within a specified time, or five painters may be needed for a construction activity.

The difficulty is that resources are not always equally productive, and doubling the number of persons may not reduce the duration by half. This problem also affects effort-driven activities. Adding resources to shorten the duration only works when the work can be subdivided into smaller packages that can be worked in parallel. Painting a room can be subdivided into the four walls and ceiling, and five (or more) persons could be working at once. Adding more resources cannot shorten activities in which the details must be accomplished in series. Substituting more productive resources or increasing the workday would be required to shorten these.

On the surface this situation seems analogous to the effort-driven model, but conceptually it is different. Usually, the customer or sponsor has established total project duration, or delivery of a product is required on a certain date. The schedule is established by fitting the activities into the available time. Resources are assigned to match the activity durations, and a trial-and-error process (including a lot of experience) is used to balance required activity durations and resources.

2. Non-Time-Critical Activities. In the second case, the activity durations are established to fit a specified project duration, but many are longer than required considering the nature of the work or the number of person-hours actually required or estimated.

The noncritical items could include an activity such as writing a test plan. The actual writing may be estimated to take only approximately 40 hours, but three weeks are shown on the schedule. The person is assigned one-third of his or her time to the activity, or 40 hours. When in the three weeks the person works on the report is not considered important as long as he or she finishes by the due date and does not spend more than 40 hours. This gives workers the flexibility to support more than one project and to balance their own workloads. This approach is the antithesis of critical chain project management (see Appendix B).

3. Master Schedule Activities. A master schedule is the top-level schedule for a project that contains the project deliverables and the summary time spans for the major project activities. It also includes major milestones established by the customer or the project manager and any major interfaces among organizations.

Many of the activities in a master schedule are the equivalent of time budgets, and the organization responsible is expected to complete all the work within the specified time span. Summary activities that span and include two or more activities are sometimes referred to as "hammock" activities. Master schedules often are composed primarily of hammock activities because they focus on interfaces among organizations and major milestones.

This is illustrated in Figure 2.19. The name originally came from the use of this type of summary activity when drawing logic networks using Activity-on-Arrow (A-O-A) or PERT networks. The A-O-A symbology is illustrated as "Normal Activities."

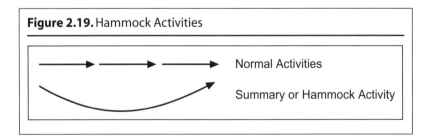

Figure 2.19. Hammock Activities

Normal Activities

Summary or Hammock Activity

For example, an organization such as "engineering" is assigned (and agrees) to perform a WBS element or a work package, such as for the design of a major assembly, within a certain period of time. This time period is reflected in the master schedule Gantt chart as a single bar (a hammock activity). The engineering organization, performing its internal planning and considering resource availability and other project commitments, develops detailed schedules of the work to be performed in the design of the components that comprise the assembly and its design. Similarly, the manufacturing and procurement organizations develop detailed schedules of the effort in their assigned work packages within the time spans of the summary activities on the master schedule.

PERT-Time Estimates

The two previous sections describe different philosophies for determining the duration of activities for planning and scheduling when using a single time estimate. This section discusses using the PERT algorithm and network planning approach to estimate activity duration. First introduced in 1958, this approach is rarely used today for planning and scheduling; it is commonly used, however, in performing risk analyses.

In the PERT concept, activities represent the work necessary to proceed from one event to another and thus require the expenditure of time and resources. Each activity is assigned three time values:

1. Optimistic: a minimum time attainable only when unusually good performance is achieved and has no more than one chance in 100 of being lessened.

2. Most Likely: a probable time that the person best qualified to judge would reasonably expect and that would occur most often if the activity could be repeated numerous times under the same conditions.

3. Pessimistic: a maximum time that can occur only if unusually bad performance is experienced and has no more than one chance in 100 of being exceeded. The pessimistic time should reflect the possibility of initial failure and a fresh start. It is not influenced by such factors as the possibility of strikes, floods, or fires, unless hazards such as these are inherent to the activity.

Some of the basic assumptions in the estimating process are as follows:

- All three estimates are based on the same level of effort. For example, all three estimates must be based on using the same number of persons working the same number of shifts and days per week. The three estimates provide a measure of the range caused by the uncertainties in a project activity. Basing each estimate on a different level of effort would really be estimating three different plans.

- The time estimates for each activity should be made or approved by the individual responsible for the work performed in the activity.

- The estimates must be determined independently of other network activities. Whether or not predecessor activities are more or less uncertain is not relevant.

The expected duration of an activity is based on a formula:

$$t_e = (a + 4m + b)/6,$$

where
a is the optimistic estimate
m is the most likely time, and
b is the pessimistic estimate.

In addition, a variance determination is made in which the variance is defined as: $\sigma 2 = (b - a)\, 2/36$. The variance is a measure of the dispersion or spread of the estimate, which can be added to make certain statistical statements regarding the likelihood of meeting project time estimates.[21]

3.2. Develop a Logic Network and Schedule

It is much easier to use project management software for network planning than to do it manually. The process is very simple; again, the key is to use the WBS as the framework.

As a first step, enter the WBS into the software using the Gantt display, as illustrated in Figure 2.20. The next step is to define the activities under each lowest WBS element—the work package per Figure 2.18. With a little practice, the activities can be defined faster than a normal person can type; in a very short time all the activities on the project will have been defined. This assumes, of course, that there is a complete WBS for the project. While the activities are being defined, it is possible to combine Step 3.2, Develop a Logic Network and Schedule with Step 3.1, Estimate Activity Duration, and Step 3.3, Assign and Schedule Resources and Costs, and perform the steps concurrently.

All project management software packages can link the activities to each other where relationships exist using any of the four different activity relationship possibilities, as shown in Figure 2.21. This figure shows what the computer is doing when different linkages are identified.

There are usually at least two methods of actually linking the activities in the computer: identifying the predecessor activity numbers or dragging with the mouse.

Manual Development of the Logic Networks

The following steps are involved in developing a network manually following the precedence or critical-path approach typical of most project management computer programs.[22]

- Activities are shown as rectangles: the left end represents the start of the activity and the right end represents the completion of the activity. The size or shape of the rectangle has no significance.

Figure 2.20. WBS Elements and Activities in MS Project 98®

AUTOMATED ORDERING SYSTEM (AOS) PROJECT

ID	WBS	Task Name	Duration
1	1	**Project Management**	**49 days**
2	1.1	**Project Start**	**49 days**
3	1.1.1	Go Ahead	0 days
4	1.1.2	Complete Project	0 days
5	1.2	**Project Meetings**	**25 days**
6	1.2.1	Prepare for Kickoff Meeting	4 hrs
7	1.2.2	Start Kickoff Meeting	0 days
8	1.2.3	Prepare for Interim Status Meeting	3 days
9	1.2.4	Start Interim Status Meeting	0 days
10	1.3	**Project Reports**	**2 days**
11	1.3.1	Prepare Interim Progress Report	2 days
12	1.3.2	Deliver Interim Progress Report	0 days
13	2	**AOS REQUIREMENTS SPECIFICATION**	**10 days**
14	2.1	**INITIAL AOS REQUIREMENTS SPECIFICATION**	**10 days**
15	2.1.1	Create Initial AOS Rqmts Spec	5 days
16	2.1.2	Review Initial AOS Reqmts Spec	2 days
17	2.1.3	Update Initial AOS Reqmts Spec	3 days
18	2.2	**FINAL AOS REQUIREMENTS SPECIFICATION**	**3 days**
19	2.2.1	Review Final AOS Reqmts Spec	2 days
20	2.2.2	Approve Final AOS Reqmts Spec	1 day
21	2.2.3	Deliver AOS Requirements Specification	0 days
22	3	**AOS DESIGN SPECIFICATION**	**17 days**
23	3.1	**INITIAL AOS DESIGN SPECIFICATION**	**13 days**
24	3.1.1	Create Initial AOS Design Spec	7 days
25	3.1.2	Review Initial AOS Design Spec	3 days
26	3.1.3	Update Initial AOS Design Spec	3 days
27	3.2	**FINAL AOS DESIGN SPECIFICATION**	**4 days**
28	3.2.1	Review Final AOS Design Spec	2 days
29	3.2.2	Approve Final AOS Design Spec	2 days
30	3.2.3	Deliver AOS Design Specification	0 days
31	4	**AOS SOFTWARE**	**25 days**
32	4.1	**AOS MODULE 1**	**20 days**
33	4.1.1	Code AOS Module 1	15 days
34	4.1.2	Unit Test AOS Module 1	5 days
35	4.2	**AOS MODULE 2**	**20 days**
36	4.2.1	Code AOS Module 2	15 days
37	4.2.2	Unit Test AOS Module 2	5 days
38	4.3	**INTEGRATE MODULES**	**5 days**
39	4.3.1	System Test Integrated Modules	5 days
40	4.3.2	Complete AOS Software	0 days

Timeline columns: January (2/1, 2/2, 2/3), (1/6, 1/13, 1/20, 1/27), February (2/3, 2/10, 2/17, 2/24), March (3/3, 3/10, 3/17, 3/24)

Milestone markers: 1/2, 3/11 (Complete Project), 1/2 (Start Kickoff Meeting), 2/5 (Start Interim Status Meeting), 1/31 (Deliver Interim Progress Report), 1/15 (Deliver AOS Requirements Specification), 2/4 (Deliver AOS Design Specification), 3/11 (Complete AOS Software)

Figure 2.21. Task Relationships

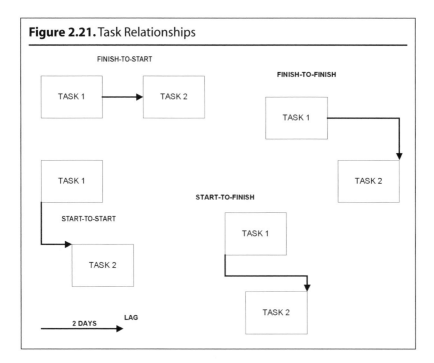

- The arrows between the activities identify only the activity relationships; they do not represent work being accomplished.

- The usual connections are from the end of one activity to the start of dependent, succeeding activities.

- Connections can be made from the start of one activity to the start of another or from the finish of one activity to the finish of another. This illustrates interdependent activities proceeding in parallel, known as partial dependencies.

- Dependency arrows do not normally indicate the use of time and are of zero duration. However, if a time lag is to be scheduled or expected between two activities, the appropriate time duration should be added to the dependency.

- Activity durations are estimated and indicated for each activity on the network. The units—days, hours, weeks, months, or minutes—are a matter of choice. All units are working time, not calendar time.

- Milestones are shown as zero-duration activities.

The four types of relationships among activities, as illustrated in Figure 2.21, are:

1. *Finish-to-Start (FS)*—the most common when the succeeding activity cannot start until the preceding activity has been completed. (This is the default linkage in project management software.)

2. *Finish-to-Finish (FF)*—occurs when the succeeding activity cannot finish until the preceding activity has been completed. The two activities may finish together.

3. *Start-to-Start (SS)*—occurs when the succeeding activity cannot start until the preceding activity has started. The two activities may start simultaneously.

4. *Start-to-Finish (SF)*—occurs when the succeeding activity's finish is based on the start of a preceding activity.

In Figure 2.21, it is assumed that the left edge of the activity box represents the start and the right edge represents the finish. It is not correct to show the linkages from the horizontal centers of the boxes because the relationship is then ambiguous.

In addition, Figure 2.21 shows another symbol in the lower left-hand corner. It is occasionally useful to show a "lag" between the start and finish of a set of tasks or to constrain start-to-start tasks. In these cases, a lag is incorporated into the arrow connecting the tasks to reflect the condition being established by the planner. Individual software packages have different mechanisms for incorporating lag.

The need to develop actual logic networks manually has disappeared as the project management software has improved. All the linkages and relationships are identified within the computer and the necessary calculations are performed immediately.

The important rule is to make sure all the predecessors are identified for each activity, recognizing that some activities may be constrained by more than one other activity or may in turn constrain multiple activities.

A "start" milestone or equivalent should be shown under the project management WBS and that all activities that are able to begin when this occurs should be linked to it. If the start date is changed, only one date needs to be changed in the computer and the entire network, and therefore the schedule, will be shifted as required.

In addition, a default duration of zero or one day should be used for all activities while developing the schedule This makes it easy to identify activities with durations that have not yet been estimated. Also, it makes it easy to identify activities with predecessors that have not yet been identified and linked since they all will be shown at "time now" or "start," depending on how the software has been instructed. Some have discovered that when using the software, it is easier to estimate activity durations prior to linking, which means combining Steps 3.1 and 3.2.

In Figure 2.20, the data of Figure 2.18 have been entered into MS Project 98® to illustrate the use of the WBS as an outline for developing the activities and structuring the schedule. Note that the WBS elements are in bold and the related activities are indented under the lowest WBS elements. Linkages are shown on the Gantt display but can be hidden to print a cleaner looking document.

Schedules are frequently prepared and issued in Gantt chart format, illustrated in Figure 2.22, or in the more sophisticated computer output of Figure 2.20.[23]

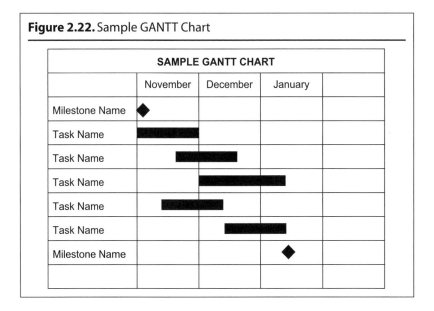

Figure 2.22. Sample GANTT Chart

SAMPLE GANTT CHART				
	November	December	January	
Milestone Name	◆			
Task Name	▬▬			
Task Name		▬▬		
Task Name		▬▬		
Task Name		▬		
Task Name		▬▬		
Milestone Name			◆	

Logic Network Calculations

The use of project management software has greatly simplified the process of calculating the networks to determine such values as the project duration, longest or most critical paths, and the amount of float or slack on noncritical paths. With project management software, the computer now performs this tedious operation almost instantaneously.[24]

Although there are very few situations in which a person might need to perform the calculations used to determine the schedule features of the project, the early terminology and abbreviations have carried over and are used by most computer programs. These are presented in the Figure 2.23.

Figure 2.23. Logic Network Calculation Terms

Early Start (ES)—the earliest time an activity can start considering the logic constraints and activity durations.
Early Finish (EF)—the earliest time an activity can finish considering the logic constraints and activity durations.
Late Start (LS)—the latest time an activity can start and not affect the calculated total duration of the project.
Late Finish (LF)—the latest time an activity can finish and not affect the calculated total duration of the project.
Critical Path—the longest path through the network.
Float or Slack—the amount of time an activity can move without affecting the total project duration.

3.3. Assign and Schedule Resources and Costs

There are three purposes for Step 3.3:

1. Determine the quantity and timing for particular types of labor resources required to support the project.

2. Develop a "bottom-up" cost estimate for the project.

3. Develop a baseline for cost control.

The first purpose provides the information necessary to identify when, what type of, and what quantity of labor resources are required and to let the appropriate persons know. Larger projects may require hiring or using temporary personnel to meet the needs. Smaller projects and smaller organizations frequently identify specific persons by name or initials (especially key personnel) to be able to identify exactly when they are required. The software also permits vacation schedules to be entered for individuals.

The second purpose is important when determining the estimated cost of the project.

The third purpose is important if tight cost control is required and it is an important component of the management of the project. All cost items, such as travel, materials, and vendor items, are identified to specific activities. The final budget data are negotiated with the supporting organizations and then "baselined."

> A "baseline" is an approved plan for an aspect of the project that is used as a basis for project control, project change control, and in this case, cost or budget.

The procedure for each activity is the same: identify or estimate the resources required to perform the activity—and repeat for *every* activity. There is no shortcut. However, there is a methodology that makes the effort simpler. Set up a resource table and assign the resources to each activity by selecting the resource from the table using your computer and project management software.

Resource Tables

When using a computer to assist in the planning and when activity durations are estimated, the resources to be assigned to the activity are usually estimated at the same time. Activity durations and resource requirements are closely related in most activities. Resource requirements are estimated in person-hours or as a percentage of a resource's time.

> A broad definition of "resource" would be something that can be drawn upon for aid. This would include labor resources, material resources, and any other items needed to accomplish the work on an activity.

A useful tool for assigning resources to activities is a resource table, such as the one illustrated in Figure 2.24. Even if analyzing and planning manually, such a table is useful for consolidating resource data.

Figure 2.24. Simplified Resource Table

RESOURCE NAME	TYPE	QUANTITY AVAILABLE	COST RATE
Project Manager	Labor	1	$70.00 per hour
Architect	Labor	1	$60.00 per hour
Cabinets (Subcontract)	Fixed Cost	1 Set	$4,000 per kitchen
Roofing Contractor	Fixed Cost—Lump Sum	1	$3,000.00 per roof
Masons	Labor	2	$30.00 per hour
Automobile Travel	Unit Cost		$0.38 per mile
Plywood	Unit Cost		$25.00 per sheet
Laborers	Labor	5	$15.00 per hour
Paint	Unit Cost		$45.00 per gallon
Rental Car	Time Cost		$50.00 per day
Programmer A	Labor	4	$70.00 per hour
Admin. Assistant	Labor (Overhead)	2	$0.00 per hour
Publishing	Unit Cost		$15.00 per page
IT Specialist	Labor	5	$45.00 per hour

Project management software programs contain a resource table similar to Figure 2.24 that needs to have appropriate data added if resources or costs are to be managed. It may contain many more data elements than the basic table and can include subcontractors. It is either prepared in advance or developed while identifying and estimating the resources assigned to each activity. In organizations performing resource planning across projects, all the project managers and administrators use a common resource pool for labor. In these situations, the table often specifies names of personnel working on the projects. The Human Resources department uses these planning data to assist in overall enterprise personnel planning.

The resources to be used by *each* activity or each work package need to be identified to develop a total cost estimate or a total resource plan. There are no shortcuts. It is not very difficult, but it can be tedious on a large project.

The way it works is very simple. Select the activity, such as "1.3.1, Prepare Interim Progress Report" in Figure 2.20, and then click on whatever icon or method will bring up the resource table. Then simply select the resource and identify its quantity, which depends on the resource units. If the project manager will prepare the progress report and will work on it full time for the duration estimated for the activity, then simply identify "1" for the quantity. If the project manager is to spend half the time on the progress report, identify "0.5" for the quantity, or simply put in the estimated hours. (This figure may depend on the particular software package and the format of your data.) The computer will determine the number of hours and the labor cost for that activity.

If there is a publishing cost for the report, add the "publishing" resource to the activity and identify the estimated number of pages. The computer will provide a total cost for the activity and roll the activity cost up the WBS to provide the total cost of the project.

Similarly, all activities are selected in turn and the necessary resources identified and assigned. All project management computer programs have the capability to add resources to the resource table at any time so the table is developed as the planning and estimating proceeds.

One person should not do all the estimating. Team participation is preferable, and those WBS elements or activities assigned to a particular organization should be estimated by that organization.

Some companies use a form that is filled out by the supervisor responsible for each activity or work package.

The form identifies the labor and cost elements and the duration of the effort. This also can also be accomplished online.

For personnel planning and scheduling, the time required of persons not charging their costs to the project but who are needed for it also needs to be identified. This would include the administrative assistant in Figure 2.24. This is shown with a $0.00 cost rate in the table.

In many organizations the labor dollar costs are not planned and tracked, but labor hours are tracked, so the cost rate also is $0.00.

For small projects, the WBS may be structured by SOW task and the resources simply estimated at the task level.

The purpose of the "Quantity Available" column in Figure 2.24 is to allow the computer or the manager to identify when resources are overcommitted or overscheduled. This is discussed under "histograms."

Once the required resources and cost elements for all the activities have been estimated, the total cost (see Step 3.4) can be calculated as well as the planned assignment of personnel. It is not unusual in the first iteration for resource conflicts and overloading to occur and for the total cost and overall duration to exceed targets. The project then needs to be replanned and re-estimated as necessary to fit within the given constraints. If this is not possible, then the scope or project objectives may need to be changed.

Anyone with some computer experience will recognize that reports can be generated if the data are in the computer system. Any items in the resource table, therefore, can be totaled. Because the data are spread by time in the logic network, time-phased data also are available.

Resource Histograms

A useful tool for presenting and analyzing resource loading on a project is the resource histogram. Histograms are used to identify graphically where individual resources are overloaded (or underused) so that appropriate adjustments to the plan can be accomplished and the person-power "smoothed." In the example illustrated in Figure 2.25, Marcia has no assignments on the project on June 1 and is assigned half time on June 2 and 3 and full time on June 4 through 8. She is overloaded on June 9 through 12 (cross hatch) and then back to half time on June 15. Nonwork days are shown in diagonal shading.

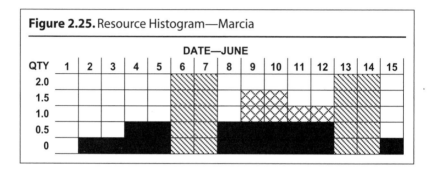

Figure 2.25. Resource Histogram—Marcia

This situation arises because Marcia is assigned work on two or more activities that are scheduled to be performed on the same date. These activities may be in the same project or in different projects. The latter occurs in the more sophisticated organizations at higher project management maturity levels where resource planning is performed across projects working from a resource pool.

With these data and the data identifying the activities Marcia is assigned to on June 9 through 12, appropriate changes in plans or assignments can be made. The project management software will identify the activities that are causing overallocation so that appropriate adjustments to the plans can be made.

Resource Leveling

One of the early capabilities and advantages in the use of the logic networks (described in Section 3.2) was the ability to identify overallocation and to perform "resource leveling." In the resource histogram shown in Figure 2.25, Marcia is overloaded on June 9, 10, 11, and 12. How can this problem be resolved?

There are two common solutions to overallocation. The first is to delay one of the activities until the overcommitted resource has time to work on it, and the second is to split the activity so that part of the activity is performed when planned and the rest is performed later when the person has time.

Other methods can also be used to balance the resource workload. The methods you choose to reduce overallocations depend on the limitations of your project, including budget, resource availability, finish date, and the amount of flexibility available for scheduling activities. It may be easy to hire another "Marcia," for example, or to reassign someone from another project.

This activity can be performed manually, or project software can do it using the resource-leveling feature that virtually all project management software contains. (A note of caution: Make sure you understand the algorithm the software uses so you can judge how to use the resulting information.) A combination of the two is the customary approach.

In most cases, overallocated resources are leveled only after all information about activity scheduling and resource availability has been entered. The computer is used to level resources, the results are reviewed, and then activity, assignment, and resource information are adjusted as necessary.

So what does the computer do? When the algorithm in the project management software levels your resources, it goes through a series of decisions about each of the activities in your logic network to determine whether they can be delayed or split to alleviate the resource overallocations. The following factors are examined to determine which activities should be delayed or split:

• Available slack or float

• Activity duration

• Activity constraints and dependencies

• Fixed schedule dates.

The software also considers resource information in the leveling process:

• Resource availability as shown in the computer analysis of the current and other ongoing projects

• Resource availability as shown by maximum units available in the pool for that particular resource

• Resource assignment units on the activity.

The computer simply uses slack or float to shift activities in time to eliminate overallocations where possible. If there is no slack or float, it will shift a lower priority activity into the future until there is no conflict, assuming you have assigned priority numbers to the activities. The computer also will check the resource pools for unassigned comparable resources.

For most projects with resource overcommitments, the first computer leveling run causes "sticker shock" and you have to go back and look more closely at your input data.

When entering schedule information for your activities, make sure you follow the requirements for the software and understand the implications of some of your decisions if you use leveling. For example, if you identify certain activities or milestones as fixed in time, they will not be adjusted by the computer, which will affect the solution provided.

The resource-leveling algorithms for the various software programs all operate differently, so you must read the manual to understand what is happening. Fortunately, they all have the option to remove or undo the leveling. For example, you may want to level only selected resources or those shared across multiple projects. The different programs also display the leveled and nonleveled activities differently and allow you to choose the order in which activities are delayed.

One of the most tedious and onerous project planning tasks is eliminating overallocated resources while at the same time trying to keep to a fixed end date for the project. You have to take one activity at a time when there is a conflict and do one of the following:

- Accept the recommendation of the computer leveling algorithm and add appropriate delays or lags between activities to match the leveled adjustments.

- Change the type or quantity (or both) of resources assigned to an activity.

- Replace an overallocated resource with an underallocated one.

- Redefine the activities to change the resource requirements.

- Modify the basic plan or statement of work.

Other conflicts may occur as you make these changes. You just have to fix all the problems.

3.4. Develop the Cost Estimate

Cost estimating is a broad field of study. This is especially true for new or unique projects for which the art and science of parametric cost estimating is required. The Association for the Advancement of Cost Engineering International (www. aacei.org) is a good reference source for advanced techniques and application of these methodologies.

For our purposes, cost estimating is based on the methodology of Steps 3.1 through 3.3.

In Step 3.1 we identified activities and their durations in the computer using project management software. For example, an activity may be: "Attend a Project Review Meeting in Atlanta," where you are one of the persons on the agenda. The activity duration is three days; you are attending 100 percent of the time, as is another member of your organization; and you are traveling from Chicago. You would identify yourself and your associate in the computer at 100 percent (or three person days or 24 person hours); you also would include travel costs such as estimated airfare, lodging, meals, and local transportation. Because the computer has a labor rate table already incorporated that includes each person's labor rate, it can calculate the labor costs and the other direct costs for this activity, as shown in Figure 2.26.

Figure 2.26. Sample Activity Cost Estimate

Cost Item	Hours	Labor Rate	Cost
Project Manager	24	$50.00 per hour	$1,200.00
Technical Director	24	$40.00 per hour	$960.00
Airfare (2 persons)			$1,000.00
Hotel (2 persons)			$600.00
Meals (2 persons)			$200.00
Local Transportation			$150.00
		Total Direct Cost	$4,110.00

This is the "bottom-up" method of cost estimating. Cost data for every activity would be similarly estimated, and the computer will rapidly calculate the cost. Because of the long duration scheduled for some activities, or because of multitasking, some persons may be assigned only part time. Not every activity would have as much data input required as in Figure 2.26. Most have only two data elements: the name of the resource and the hours or the percentage of the person's time.

The importance of the 100 percent rule described earlier becomes apparent when developing the WBS, which makes sure all the activities are identified and, therefore, 100 percent of the costs as well.

You immediately have some questions:

a. Isn't this a lot of work?

b. How can we estimate to this level of detail when putting together a proposal or the first plan when we haven't done the preliminary work yet?

c. Where do I get the data on activities others are going to work on?

d. How do I handle the financial data such as overhead rates, general and administrative (G&A) rates, and fee?

e. How about inflation?

f. Our organization only works for other internal organizations, so we are not concerned about overhead rates. How does this impact the methodology?

g. What level of detail is needed?

h. What level of accuracy is needed?

a. Amount of Work—Too many books on project management gloss over the work required or provide "silver bullets" that supposedly will reduce the work. Effective project management is work, it requires detail, and there are no shortcuts to the basic activities. The biggest change in the past 20 years is the advent of excellent computer software and hardware. However, computer software assists only in organizing, processing, and displaying data—it does not think for you. If you follow the methodology, however, software organizes the steps logically and thereby simplifies the process.

With experience and learning, each project will go more smoothly, but each requires work.

There isn't any free lunch. If it were simple or easy, you wouldn't be needed!

b. Level of Detail (Proposal or Initial Plan)—The task of putting together the first cost estimate or project plan seems daunting. You will be surprised by how much you or your organization already knows. To begin with, you would not be putting together a proposal or an initial work plan if you did not already know something about the work in the project (or if your supervisor did not think you could do it). (See also paragraph g on level of detail.)

c. Gathering Data on Activities—To acquire the data on activities others will work on, you may need to meet with the key people and discuss each activity, which persons will be working on each activity, and what work will be done. The process is easier if a work statement has been prepared that tracks to the WBS and the schedule or activity plan in the computer. However, you can use the project management software, project it on a screen, and get the inputs directly from the persons in the audience or work online. Or you can provide hard copy of the detailed schedule and copy the activity list from the software, such as MS Project®, and transfer it to Excel™. Using a laptop, project it onto the screen, add columns to represent the labor and cost categories, and have members of the team estimate the labor and costs for each activity.

Figure 2.27 offers two alternate abbreviated versions of the array. Data would be entered only for the activities, in this example in those rows without WBS numbers. Additional columns would be added to match the specific resource breakdown of the organization and project. Additional rows would be added so that all WBS elements and their supporting activities can be identified.

Most organizations use one format or the other and set up a template to use for each project. Data are then transferred to the project management software or kept in a spreadsheet, depending on how they will be used in the later phases of the project.

> Bottom-up cost estimating is performed using the WBS and activity list as the structure. Layout can vary with the organization and project.

d. Overhead Rates, G&A Rates, and Fee—There are at least three answers for question "d." Many organizations have a finance department or a person responsible for putting together the final cost estimate who will apply the appropriate overhead rates to arrive at the total price. Policy and competitive strategy determines the fee. The project office often is asked to estimate only labor hours and direct costs, such as in the array in Figure 2.27a, and the Finance Department takes care of these items. However, it is important for the project manager to understand how these items are determined and their impact on the price. The three methods are as follows:

Method 1: Use of a Standard, Specified Format—Figure 2.28 shows another common format used to summarize and present the cost estimate for a project.

Figure 2.27a. Partial Cost Estimating Array, Spreadsheet Model, Layout A

A	B	C	D	E	F	G	H	I	J
1					Organization Hours				
2									
3	WBS		A	B	C	D	E	F	TOTAL
4	1	PROJECT MANAGEMENT							
5	1.1	Project planning							
6		Gather preliminary data							
7		Update master schedule							
8		Assessment preliminary planning							
9	1.2	Meetings							
10		Project kickoff meeting							
11		Assessment kickoff meeting							
12		In Progress Reviews							
13		IPR 1							
14		IPR 2							
15		IPR 3							
16	1.3	Status reports							
17		Status reports 1							
18		Status reports 2							
19		Status reports 3							
20	2	PM MATURITY ASSESSMENT							
21	2.1	Preparation							
22		Load special PM assess SW							
23		ETC.							
24		TOTAL HOURS							
25		Cost Estimates							
26		Total labor effort by organization							
27		Labor rate							
28		Total labor cost by organization							
29		Materials							
30		Hardware							
31		Software							
32		Miscellaneous							
33		Travel							
34		Other direct costs							
35		Management reserve (10%)							
36		TOTAL COST							

Figure 2.27b. Partial Cost Estimating Array, Spreadsheet Model, Layout B

A	B	C	D	E	F	G	H	I	J
1				Labor Hours			Costs ($)		
2			Project	Senior		IT			
3	WBS		Manager	Analyst	Analyst	Specialist	Materials	Pubs	Travel
4									
5	1.1	Process alignment							
6		Process alignment planning							
7		Process capture and mapping							
8		Process gap analysis							
9	1.2	Data migration and cutover							
10		Data migration and cutover planning							
11		Data migration algorithm and scripts							
12		Data cutover rehearsals							
13		Rehearsal 1							
14		Rehearsal 2							
15		Rehearsal 3							
16		Production data cutover							
17	1.3	Training							
18		Training planning							
19		Development and validation of training materials							
20	1.4	Etc.							
21		Business simulation testing							
22	1.9	Etc.							
23		Project management							
24		TOTAL							

Figure 2.28. Cost Proposal Format

Date:			COST PROPOSAL		
			SAMPLE PROJECT NUMBER 34		
DIRECT LABOR					
		HOURLY	ESTIMATED	ESTIMATED	
		RATE	HOURS	COST	
Project Director		$60.00	40	$2,400.00	
Technical Director		$55.00	400	$22,000.00	
Systems Analyst		$40.00	20	$800.00	
Database Administrator		$25.00	700	$17,500.00	
			TOTAL DIRECT LABOR COST		$42,700.00
FRINGE BENEFITS:		33.00%	of TOTAL DIRECT LABOR (TDL)		$14,091.00
				LABOR SUBTOTAL	$56,791.00
LABOR OVERHEAD		20.00%	of TDL PLUS FRINGE		$11,358.20
			TOTAL LABOR COSTS		$68,149.20
OTHER DIRECT COSTS (ODC)					
		Telephone and fax		$1,600.00	
		Material and supplies		$1,500.00	
		Publication costs		$1,800.00	
			TOTAL ODC		$4,900.00
CONSULTANT COSTS		80 hours @ $75.00 per hour			$6,000.00
SUBCONTRACT COSTS		Company Super, Inc.			$10,000.00
TRAVEL					$5,234.00
		SUBTOTAL: LABOR, ODC & TRAVEL			$94,283.20
GENERAL AND ADMINISTRATIVE					
		9.00% of SUBTOTAL			$8,485.49
		TOTAL COST			$102,768.68
FEE		7.00%			$7,193.81
		TOTAL PRICE			**$109,962.48**
Standard Form 60					

Many U.S. government organizations request that this format or one similar be used to provide cost data in a response to a solicitation. (See Scenario 4, Part 3.) The basic input data are provided by the project management software in summary form and entered into the model at the appropriate place.

Note that three different overhead rates are used, and note the order in which they are applied. The example has a "fringe benefits," "labor overhead," and "general and administrative" rate. Often the fringe benefits and the labor overhead are combined into one rate. Figure 2.29 defines these rates. The direct labor rate (e.g., the $60.00 per hour for the project director) is the actual amount the person would see in his or her paycheck before any deductions.

Figure 2.29. Overhead Rate Definitions

Fringe benefits	Costs that include retirement, FICA, medical and dental, Medicare, and any other items that relate directly to the employee
Labor overhead	Costs to the employer that relate to the working environment, such as cleaning, building costs, parking lot expenses, lighting, water, and sewage
General and administrative	Costs that relate to running the enterprise, such as the corporate-level staff, marketing, the CEO, Board expenses, and corporate offices

The actual rate that is used (e.g., the 33%, 20%, or 9%) are all determined similarly.
The estimated or actual costs of the total fringe benefits pool for the enterprise organization of the project (e.g., the division of the organization) are divided by the total direct labor costs of the division including all projects.
The estimated or actual costs of the labor overhead pool are determined similarly, except that the base includes the fringe benefit costs.
The general and administrative rate includes the total costs attributed to the corporate-level activities divided by the total direct, fringe, and labor overhead costs of the enterprise.

Figure 2.29 illustrates how the overhead rates are applied to build the cost. Note also that for direct costs such as sub-contracts, consultants, materials, and supplies, only G&A rates are applied. That is because the labor required to acquire these items is already accounted for in the direct labor or the labor overhead pool. These costs do go into the G&A pool used to determine the G&A rate.

Many more aspects of these rates may be relevant. For example, some overhead cost items could be either in the labor overhead or the G&A overhead, and there are some rules for determining this. Also, in companies that do business with the government, the government reviews, audits, and approves the methods of calculation. As a project manager, you need to understand what these rates are and how they affect the cost estimate.

It is important to realize that overhead costs, *over which you have no control,* may in some organizations exceed the costs that are directly related to the project. Allowing overhead rates to get too high could make your organization noncompetitive on price.

Similarly, assigning too many highly paid but less productive persons to your project could make you non-competitive. It is tough being a project manager in a private-sector organization where you have to compete for business.

If you and your project are in a federal, state, or local government organization, you do not normally need to be concerned about the overhead rates and the salaries of the members of the project team. Your problem usually centers on getting good resources of any kind.

A final consideration is the fee or profit. The size of the fee in your initial estimate is determined partially by the market, partially by your higher management, and partially by the risk inherent in the project and the terms of the contract.

Fixed-price or lump-sum contracts in which the project and the enterprise bear all the financial risk justify larger fees than do cost contracts in which the customer bears the cost risk. These are normally negotiable, and your finance manager or higher-level managers can provide information regarding your project, if necessary.

Method 2. Use of Project Management Software—The second method used to account for overhead, G&A, and fee in the price is to include these items in all the labor rates and cost elements and thereby arrive at a total price. Some project management software will allow you to enter the direct labor and overhead rates in a basic data table and will then calculate the costs with those factors. You still have to estimate the number of hours each resource is planned to spend on each activity.

It is mostly upscale software that has the capability to accommodate multiple overhead rates. Some organizations have written their own computer programs to develop the complete cost estimate from the output of the project management software. If your organization has less sophisticated software and you wish to use the project management software and not the spreadsheet approach, a partial solution would be to enter burdened rates (i.e., rates with overhead included) into the labor rate tables so that the software will provide total labor costs. ("Add-ons" are available for some project management software to help generate cost estimates including overhead rates.)

Cost data also must be increased by the G&A rate to keep the labor and direct cost data compatible. For example, the fully burdened rate for the project director in Figure 2.28 is $60.00 x 1.33 x 1.20 x 1.09 x 1.07 = $60.00 x 1.86 = $111.60 per hour. (Multipliers of 2.0–2.5 and higher are common in some industries, especially those with offices located in expensive downtown districts of large cities.) This is the rate that would need to be entered into MS Project®, for example, to calculate total prices for labor. Other cost elements also would need to include G&A and fee rates in their totals.

Method 3. Use of PM Software and a Comprehensive Cost Model—The third method is to use the project management software to define the scope of the project and to identify all the activities in a WBS framework. Modify the spreadsheet to incorporate all the different rates and fee into the array, and convert it into a complete cost estimating model. The rates and the calculations shown in Figure 2.28 are incorporated into the model at the top along the "x" axis and the WBS activities copied from the PM software on the left along the "y" axis. The resulting model will look like Figure 2.27b, except that there will be many more columns along the "x" axis to accommodate the calculations.

e. Inflation—Inflation or price level increases from any cause are a problem for project managers who must control costs of multiyear projects. They have only limited options. One is to include a price-level index in your contract or charter (if you have one) where automatic adjustments are made to contract prices under certain conditions.

The second option is to estimate and build in expected price level increases carefully in each area likely to be affected. For example, costs of certain materials may be expected to increase faster than certain labor costs.

For multiyear projects, the recommended approach is to estimate all costs in "constant dollars" (e.g., year 2005), and then use the project management software and schedule to identify which activities are performed in each year. Change the estimated dollars in each year to "current dollars" by multiplying the estimates by the expected price level increases from the base year. Current dollars take into consideration price level increases, sometimes referred to as inflation increases.

Finally, set aside a certain amount for contingency—a management reserve to provide a cushion. Talk to your sponsor or customer about this factor and agree in advance how it will be accommodated and who will bear the risk.

f. Supporting Other Internal Organizations—If your organization works only for other internal organizations or does not have to recover total costs, the methodology is still applicable. You still need to have an estimate of the resources needed to support the project. The best way is to make sure that all activities are identified, consider the work in each activity, and estimate the number of person hours of each skill (or percentage of time) and other costs.

The result is not a total price, but a list of people or skills, the number of hours you need them for a particular time period, and a total cost for purchased items. It is the same basic problem of planning and controlling costs or resources but with fewer variables and a different presentation of the requirements.

g. Level of Detail—The level of detail needed to establish the cost estimate depends on three considerations:

1. The expectations and requirements of the customer or sponsor regarding the quality of the cost estimate

2. The level of detail necessary to establish organization budgets

3. The level of detail required for effective control.

The second and third items will be dealt with in Steps 4.1 and 6.1, respectively.

Some considerations regarding the first item are:

- *The customary requirements of your organization*—What has been done on other projects? What does your management expect regarding format, level of detail, and justification?

- *The use of the estimate*—Is it going into a proposal? Will it be used as the basis for evaluating the economic viability of the project, as part of a cash-flow analysis, or as the basis for negotiating costs or for budgeting and authorizing work?

The quality of the estimate often depends on the experience of the organization in estimating the costs of similar work and on the level of detail of the cost breakdown.

Section 3.1 presents several scenarios that provide guidance regarding the level of detail at the project's start-up. As a general rule:

Prepare the WBS to as low a level of detail as possible, to the point where the work to produce the deliverable items can be identified.

Remember that the WBS does not include activities and that its lowest level is the work packages. Make sure to follow the 100 percent rule (see Step 2.1). Load the WBS into project management software. Also load all deliverables and define the activities to perform the work in the WBS and to produce the deliverable items. Identify the resources and costs necessary to perform each activity and total them, as discussed previously.

This is work; most people do not find it to be "fun," but it is essential.

The lowest level of detail may be limited by lack of definition of the product being delivered; nevertheless, you must go to the lowest level possible. More detail may be determined during later phases, depending on the type of project.

h. Level of Accuracy—The level of accuracy depends on how the estimate is to be used and the quality of the input data. Remember GIGO—garbage in, garbage out? This usually relates to the amount of effort put into generating the basic cost estimate. People generally do not like to provide estimates for two reasons: (1) estimates take time away from more interesting work and (2) people generally do not like to be held accountable for their estimates, especially in organizations in which management sanctions are imposed for not meeting estimates.

The "accuracy" of the estimate is different from determining what strategic or tactical management factors will be used to adjust the baseline estimate. This means considering market forces, funds availability, risk, history, parallel parametric analyses, return on investment and benefit-cost analyses, internal politics, etc.

3.5. Establish Checkpoints and Performance Measures
The next step in the project management methodology is establishing checkpoints and performance measures.

3.5.1. Critical Checkpoints
Every project has certain critical checkpoints (CCPs) at which major decisions are made or major milestones are reached. These are the points where management attention needs to be focused as the project is implemented. These CCPs should be identified, successful performance defined, variance limits established where relevant, and the mechanisms to measure performance relative to the CCPs established. Risk analyses often are conducted at these CCPs.

If you can find no logical or obvious CCPs, then you need to create one or more. Add "in-process reviews" (IPRs) at intermediate points. If the project is six months long, schedule one at the midpoint or schedule two of them six weeks apart. (See Step 5.3 for further discussion.)

> Many projects involving engineering development use well-defined and understood milestones such as 25 percent, 50 percent, and 90 percent drawing release; or Preliminary Design Review (PDR), Critical Design Review (CDR), or Factory Acceptance Test (FAT).

3.5.2. Variance Limits

Step 7.1 includes a discussion of determining variances and Step 8.1 includes a discussion of corrective action. Performance measurement involves determining when a variance is significant. Common sense is used, as well as knowledge of the overall status of the project. For example, a $15 overrun on a work package budgeted at $15,000 is of little concern. An overrun of $5,000 is probably of more concern. But if the $5,000 overrun is on a noncritical work package and there are larger underruns—meaning that the overall project is running under—there may be little cause for concern. Risk analysis should be used to set variance limits or ranges (see Part 4.3).

It is common to set variance limits such as +/– 10 percent on cost or person-hours to prompt an investigation into any variance exceeding this amount to determine the cause and the impact on the project. For schedule dates, critical path analyses are useful, with any items on the critical or near-critical paths that are late or forecast to be late getting immediate attention. Each project is different, and the specific activities that vary from their baseline values also vary in significance.

Other performance measures also should be developed, depending on the nature of the product and culture of the organization. Neuendorf, who discusses many different aspects of project performance measurement, states: "Much of what organizations do or want to do depends on the ability to assess actions and results quantitatively."[25] One widely used method of measuring performance on medium and larger projects is the "earned value" technique.

3.5.3. Performance Measurement Using "Earned Value"

Using the earned value management system (EVMS) can provide a continuous measure of performance of the total project or of selected areas. The application should be considered only on projects over approximately $5,000,000 in value and one to two years in duration unless the organization is experienced in the application of EVMS and has the necessary internal systems and procedures in place. EVMS is based on a relatively simple concept that involves comparing the actual cost incurred on a work package to the original budgeted cost of the same work package and comparing the planned to the actual schedule for the same work package. These are integrated and displayed in a form that enables a determination of whether the actual work performed matches the planned work and provides a predictor of the outcome of the project.

The U.S. government requires the use of EVMS on major projects.[26] The principles are described in an industry ANSI standard.[27] In addition, the Project Management Institute has established a College of Performance Management, which focuses on the application and implementation of EVMS-type performance management systems.

This important technique is discussed in more detail in Appendix B, with references in the Bibliography.

3.6. Establish Project Baselines

Once the logic network and associated resources are adjusted to meet the project's schedule requirements and cost objectives, the results can be "baselined." A baseline is defined as "an approved reference point, at a specific time, for control of future changes to a product's performance, construction, and design."[28] With common use, this definition has been extended to cover not only products but also schedules, costs estimates, and various contractual documents such as the specification or requirements. These baselines are necessary to implement programs of integrated change control.

A "budget baseline" is established at two levels. The first is the project budget, which covers the total cost or total resources of the project; in other words, the amount the project manager has to work with. The second level is the organization budgets that the project manager negotiates or assigns to the organizations supporting the project. (This second level is addressed in Step 4.1.)

3.6.1. Establishing a Multi-Dimensional Baseline

As mentioned in Section 3.3, establishing a multi-dimensional baseline often involves a lot of work just to get the resources balanced. The intent is to optimize the project plan—a complex undertaking.

Depending on the project management scenario that fits your situation, you also may be juggling schedules and costs to fit the project within its specified constraints.

As a general rule, four sets of constraints must be considered during the planning phase:

1. *Overall Project Duration*—schedule of deliverables, intermediate milestones

2. *Overall Project Budget or Funding*—availability of resources, cash flow limits, travel cost ceilings, facility limitations

3. *Quality Standards*—deliverable performance, testing requirements, customer expectations

4. *Statement of Work*—contract clauses, operating procedures.

These four items may need to be renegotiated or revised as the planning proceeds to fit within the constraints. Definable risks associated with each need to be determined and considered.

There is no easy solution or mechanism to iterate among these four items. As project manager, you will know what is most important to the customer—the outputs of the project—and you will have to work with your team to balance the inputs to match. The flexibility matrix discussed in Part 2, Step 1.3 helps present the customer's expectations and facilitates these tradeoff decisions. Sometimes you may have to go back to the customer or sponsor for changes to the SOW, deliverable schedules, performance, or budget to make the pieces fit. Or you may have to accept a higher risk than normal and establish plans to mitigate those risks.

Using project management software, you can establish a budget/resource and schedule baseline by clicking on an item in a drop-down list to establish the baseline after all the iterations have been completed. The schedule data and resource configurations are frozen but are available for comparison to actual performance. Changes to the baseline can be tracked and an audit trail produced, if desired. Actual schedule and budget documents sometimes referred to generically as "artifacts" (generally defined as an object made by human work) also should be under formal change control.

For product-type projects, the performance of the end items or deliverables is defined in a specification. The contract is signed, baselining the contract terms and conditions, and the SOW is baselined in some form or another. All the formal documents required to establish a multidimensional baseline are produced and the appropriate approvals given. These documents, including schedules and budgets, are distributed to all organizations involved in the project, and the procedures that allow changes to the baseline only under certain specified and controlled conditions are implemented.

The project manager must tightly control changes to the baselines. Other types of changes, such as actual completion dates for activities and actual resource expenditures, do not change the baseline data. Comparisons to the baseline are readily available for variance analysis, corrective action assignments, and graphic presentations. Changes to the baseline usually are accompanied by formal configuration management processes and concurred on by the project sponsor (see Part 6.6).

3.6.2. Negotiating the Project Budget

The best way to negotiate the total budget is to first have completed at least a quick pass through the methodology and thus be able to relate work packages and their costs to the statement of work. Even if the project manager is given or dictated an initial figure, it is necessary to go through the methodology steps up to this point to verify the reasonableness of that figure and the amount of risk involved. The better prepared the project manager is, the more likely he or she is to get the amount of resources needed or the better position he or she will be in to discuss eliminating work if there is a ceiling on the amount of funds available.

3.7. Develop the Project Plan[29]

For all projects, especially for projects operating in a matrix organization environment, a project plan document should be developed. This document is an extension of the project charter and contains much the same information, but in more detail because it is prepared at the end of the planning phase. Like many of the documents that support the project, it imposes discipline: it requires the project manager to focus on planning and to document the "who, what, when, where, how much, and how good" of the project.

Reasons to prepare a project plan include:

1. To guide project execution

2. To eliminate or reduce uncertainty

3. To document project planning assumptions, constraints, and decisions

4. To document functional department support commitments

5. To gain and communicate a better understanding of the project objectives

6. To provide a basis for monitoring and controlling work

7. To facilitate communications with stakeholders

8. To encourage the project manager to think out all aspects of the project.

The project plan is a formal, approved document. It is expected to change over time, as more information becomes known about the project and when changes in scope occur. Figure 2.30 is a sample outline and brief discussion of the typical contents of each section.

Figure 2.30. Sample Project Plan Outline

Title Page	Signatures of major stakeholders—especially functional managers and the sponsor/customer.
Project Charter	Update the project charter or the project manager's charter. Depending on contents of the charter, certain of the following sections may not be required.
Project Goals and Objectives	Describe the goals and objectives if they are not already defined in the project charter section. Include project justification and critical success factors.
Project Management Approach	Describe how the project will be managed, including meeting schedules, project reviews, reporting requirements and plans, tracking methodology, and customer/sponsor interface. Include communication plans with stakeholders.
WBS	Provide a detailed WBS and, if applicable, a WBS dictionary in an appendix.
Scope Statement or Statement of Work	Describe what work is planned. Organize the work by the WBS. Include detail work plan if relevant. Include a section on the project, planning, and scheduling assumptions.
OBS with Assignments or Assignment Matrix	Develop an organizational breakdown structure (OBS) to identify responsibility for work. Alternatively, prepare a responsibility assignment matrix cross-referenced to the WBS.
Resource Plan	Provide the project requirements for resources and document the commitments. This may include facilities, space, and equipment as well as key staff resources.
Master Schedule, Major Milestones and Deliverables	Include the master schedule baseline, including major milestones and deliverables. It should be in Gantt format but based on network planning.
Cost and Performance Baselines	Include budgets by organization. Identify the performance specifications if relevant—for both project and product.
Risk Management Plan	Include an identification of risk elements and the risk response plan or a plan of how risk management will be accomplished.
Quality Management Plan and Product Performance	Describe how quality assurance and quality control will be accomplished and how product performance will be verified.

continues

Figure 2.30. Sample Project Plan Outline (continued)

Communication Plan	Identification of stakeholders and their communication requirements, frequency and style of reports, team member communications and status reports, and project manager communications.
Subsidiary Plans	Include other plans or summaries of plans as required by the project environment or customer, (i.e., test plans, public relations plans, staffing management plans, development plans, training plans, procurement plans, etc.).
Change Management	Discuss the procedures for making changes to the performance and cost and schedule baselines, including project scope, and the approvals process.
Deliveries and Acceptance	Describe what needs to be done to deliver the product to the customer and describe the acceptance or test procedures.
Close Out	Describe the closeout process, requirements, and responsibilities.

There are many ways to organize the project plan, and not all the sections listed in Figure 2.30 are needed for every project. Use the outline as a checklist and adapt it to the situation. Several of the items are available from the project management software. The format and approvals usually will differ from project to project unless the organization has developed common standards to be used. The project plan does not need to be a long, complex document, and for many projects it can be relatively short.

The project plan is another project management tool that is essential for effective project management. Use of the project plan is a way of life in mature project management organizations. The title page or inside cover page should include the signatures of the major stakeholders. The project manager signs the document representing the project team, which should have participated in developing the document. The other important signatories are the heads of the functional organizations committed to support the project with resources and the sponsor or customer.

In establishing the project plan, the project manager cannot work alone. Participation is needed from affected organizations and individuals. Often during the process of coordination and approval, negotiations will be needed to resolve schedule, cost, or resource conflicts. The project manager, through negotiations, must resolve these conflicts in the best interests of the project. The important project charter provides the scope of the project manager's authority and responsibility and, therefore, grants the ability to resolve conflicts.

3.8. Approve the Project Plan

Whatever format it takes or amount of detail it contains, the project plan is a very important document. Approval of the plan signifies approval to proceed with implementing the project. Because this usually signifies the start of major expenditures on the project, it is important that the planning precede the implementation.

> In many organizations and on many projects, a major milestone occurs at the end of the planning stage: the approval to start the actual work on the project. One large company refers to this approval milestone as "going to project" and requires Board of Directors approval for large, company-funded projects. It is often a major hurdle for the project manager to get all the necessary approvals (or for a contractor to get the award) to proceed to the next phase.

C. EXECUTING STAGE

This is the stage of the overall project when the work is performed. The initiating stage gets the project started in the right direction; the planning stage is essential to define the work and when and how it will be performed. The purpose of the first two stages and the first three steps of the methodology are to prepare for this stage: executing.

The methodology starts with Step 4 and builds on the work of the planning stage.

4. Perform the Work
    4.1. Budget and authorize the work.
    4.2. Add staff resources.
    4.3. Produce results.
    4.4. Accommodate change requests.
5. Communicate and Coordinate Work
    5.1. Coordinate work.
    5.2. Prepare progress reports.
    5.3. Hold project reviews.

Step 4 of the methodology is arguably the most important, although it cannot be accomplished without Step 5 or the preceding steps. This is where the work is done to meet the project objectives. It is where most of the resources are expended and most of the costs are incurred. The milestone that precedes this phase—approval of the project plan—is especially important because beginning execution before at least a major portion of the planning is completed invites major problems. The reason is very simple: starting work—especially on large projects for which many people might be assigned or hired, or when there is a high probability that the work will change—introduces high-cost risk. A useful principle is to "baseline early; freeze late," which means to get early control of changes and manage them, freezing the configuration as late as possible to allow changes that improve the product.

During the Cold War the executing stage of many projects was started in parallel with the planning (known as "concurrent engineering") in order to complete the projects as soon as possible because of the perceived threat. The cost risk was known and accepted. Although many stories of large overruns come out of this circumstance, it was not bad management: The risks were recognized and all the appropriate project management process steps were followed.

Step 4. Perform the Work

4.1. Budget and authorize the work.
4.2. Add staff resources.
4.3. Produce results.
4.4. Accommodate change requests.

In this stage the project manager is responsible for authorizing the work, adding the necessary staff resources, producing results, and providing the deliverable items.

Koontz and O'Donnell write that the project manager also must direct the work to be performed,[30] a function different from following the project management methodology. An edited version of their description of this function of management follows:

> The executive function of direction embraces those activities which are related to guiding and supervising subordinates. Although the concept of direction is relatively simple, there is extraordinary complexity in subject matter and methods. There must be a keen appreciation of the enterprise traditions, history, objectives, and policies. They must know the organization structure and the interdepartmental relationships of activities and personalities and must become familiar with their duties and the usage of their authority. They must develop the ability to work with, and learn from, others, and, above all, must become effective leaders.

In Step 4, the first substep is to plan. Depending on the organization and internal procedures and processes for project management, preparing the budget could be part of the planning stage because a budget is a plan. This phase would start when the work is authorized.

4.1. Budget and Authorize the Work

The project manager must be given authorization to begin the work; then he or she in turn authorizes the team members or their organizations to start work on the activities comprising the project. The specific documents used for these purposes vary from organization to organization.

The first step is preparing and negotiating the operating budgets for the individual organizations that are supporting the project. The second step is providing the authorizations to do work.

4.1.1. Budgeting

A budget is another form of plan. It represents the amount of dollars or resources an organization is allowed to spend to perform specified tasks in a given period of time. There are frequently two components of the budget at the top level. One is the amount of the budget for the total project that is issued to the operating organizations or persons doing the work, and the other is the contingency or management reserve. These total up to one of the following figures, depending on the scenario (see Part 3):

- The total contract amount that has been negotiated or agreed to in the contract

- The amount your supervisor or sponsor said is available for the project, and to which you have agreed

- The amount you have estimated in the previous phase, Step 3.5, and are willing to commit to accomplish the project

- The amount you as project manager have been authorized to spend.

All of these are the same—the terminology simply varies with the scenario.

The size of the management reserve is variable and depends on an evaluation of the cost risk and the effectiveness of the cost controls. Figures ranging between 10 and 20 percent of the total project budget are common.

> The management reserve is often explicitly identified to a specific work package, and the project manager is the only person authorized to distribute this part of the project budget.

During the budgeting process, the project manager is now in the middle. He or she was responsible for getting the budget for the project and now is responsible for allocating it to the various persons or organizations that will be working on the project. Ideally, the project manager was able to get the major persons who will be working on the project to participate in any negotiations with the customer or sponsor regarding the budget. It is a rare project in which there is no negotiation regarding the total resources to be assigned or the total cost or price.

The starting point in the budgeting process is the output from the cost estimating process and any negotiated changes. These are used to update the data in the computer, where resources and costs are related to activities and organizations. Reports provide a Gantt chart of the activities for which each organization is responsible and the amount or cost of resources required for each activity and in total. These data provide the basis for the budgets assigned to each organization. The project manager now has reversed roles relative to the operating organizations. He or she must convince them that they can perform their work within the assigned resources and must obtain their agreement.

> If the project manager cannot get the supporting organizations to agree on their budgets, then he or she must try to get the project budget increased, change the SOW, or escalate the problem in the organization.

4.1.2. Work Authorization

Work authorization is a key step in the process. It is this step where control of the project can be lost.

Work authorization formats vary from organization to organization. They can be a simple verbal "okay" to proceed or they can be very formal. As with much of the methodology, this depends on the project environment and culture of the organization. The more formal the budgeting process, the more formal the work authorization.

Very simply, the work authorization is a contract between the project manager and the person or organizations providing support. On small projects in which the team members all report to the project manager, very little formality is required because the project manager may be directing the day-to-day activities, keeping track of the amount of time each person spends working on the project. However, in a matrix organization, the written work authorization becomes an important control and communication tool.

Since the work authorization is a form of contract, the following data are required:

- A statement of work or list of tasks

- The authorized dollars or person-hours

- The start and completion dates, and intermediate milestones if relevant

- The performance or quality expected of the end product, specifications, and other relevant documents

- A "charge number" (the internal accounting code or codes for the work to be performed)

• Other administrative data, including project name, title of the work, date, WBS numbers, organization, signature blocks, and revision blocks.

Obviously, the authorized dollars or person-hours must relate to the approved budgets, and the schedule dates must relate to the master schedule. It is also recommended that the signature blocks, in addition to the necessary approvals, also indicate acceptance of the work described on the form.

Note that the work authorization is not much different from the project charter discussed earlier. In fact, it is the equivalent of the charter for the organization supporting the project.

In issuing work authorizations, the project manager must take into account the size of any possible contingency or reserve. Before budgets are issued, an analysis of the work of each organization may need to be performed and a determination made of how much the project manager should retain in the reserve. Some organizations use the principle of feeding buffers or phase buffers for contingencies, adapting the principles of critical chain project management (see Appendix B).

All projects need a process for controlling changes. If formal work authorizations are issued, a formal process will be needed for amending the work authorizations as changes occur. After all, these are contracts for work to be done in the future; no matter how good the planning, unforeseen problems and opportunities arise. If a reserve has been kept, it may well be spent through changes to work authorizations.

Once an organization is issued a "charge number," the project manager must closely monitor the expenditures. One West Coast company had a very large overrun from one division. When queried, the division manager's response was: "I did not have any other number to charge the time of my people to!" After some negotiation and discussion, most of the charges were changed to "overhead," with the reluctant agreement of the division vice president.

Project managers often resent this part of the job. They believe, rightly, that this is a lot of work, and they prefer to be involved in the real work of the project and not the paperwork. This is the reason project managers have administrative assistants and project control personnel. Very simply, the larger the project, the more formal the paperwork and the more involved the project manager becomes in the management functions of planning, organizing, staffing, controlling, and coordination. It goes with the territory.

Once the project manager issues work authorizations, the team is off and running. You must have completed the planning phase. If you issue work authorizations before the work is defined, you are inviting a major overrun and late deliveries.

4.2. Add Staff Resources

Personnel are added to the project team in accordance with project plan timing and quantities authorized in the work authorizations. This should be an easy step, especially if most of the team has been involved in the planning phase and they have been waiting for the work to be authorized— for example, when the team has been working on a proposal and the work authorization occurs concurrently with contract award (see Part 3, Scenario 5).

It is important to get the project started off on the right foot. One method is to use a checklist such as that developed by Zenger-Miller.[31] The project manager chairs a meeting at which each participant is given a checklist to complete; each item is then discussed. The checklist includes asking whether or not enough information is provided to answer questions such as:

- What is the purpose of the project?

- What specifically are we to accomplish?

- What is the time frame for results?

- What is each team member's specific role?

Whether you use a checklist or any other mechanism, such as a kick-off meeting, there are many approaches described in the literature.[32] It is important to remember that, as the project manager, *you must make sure each participant understands what is expected of him or her, when it is expected, and what quality of work is expected.* This is best accomplished as each person comes on board the project and before they start work.

A frequently used tool is the responsibility assignment matrix, illustrated in Figure 2.31. (The initials of the persons on the project team are entered in the first row.)

Figure 2.31. Responsibility Assignment Matrix

WBS/Person	ABD	CEF	GHJ	AAE	RGN	BLO	WEP
1.1. Project Planning	P	A, P	P	P	P	P	P
1.2.1.1. User Registration and Role-Mapping	I	S	A	I	R	P	I
1.2.1.2. Subsidiary Alignment Support Plans	P	A	P	P	R, I	R, I	R, I
1.2.1.3. Process Capture and Mapping	I	S	P	P	P	I	A, P
1.2.2.1. Data Inventory and Conversion	I	S	P	A, P	P	P	I
1.2.2.2. PDM Schema Updates	R	S	I	A, P	I	P	I
1.2.3.1. Training Materials	A, P	S	P	R	I, P	I	P
1.2.3.2. Business Simulation Training	A, P	S	P	R	I, P	I	P
1.2.3.3. Alignment Training	A, P	S	P	R	I, P	I	P
1.2.4.1. Data Cutover Rehearsal 1	I	S	P, R	P, R	R	A, P	I
1.2.4.2. Business Simulation Testing 1	P, R	S	A, P	P, R	P, R	I	P, R
1.2.4.3. Data Cutover Rehearsal 2	I	S	P, R	P, R	R	A, P	I
1.2.4.4. Business Simulation Testing 2	P, R	S	A, P	P, R	P, R	I	P, R
1.2.5.1. Go-Live (Formal Data Cutover/Disable)	I	S	P	A, P	R	P	R
1.2.5.2. Post-Deployment Support	P, A	S	P	P	P	P	P

P = Participate, A = Accountable, R = Review, I = Input, S = Sign-off

In addition to defining and authorizing the activities to be performed, the project manager must make sure that the person assigned the activity is aware of the assignment. The project manager cannot just issue a memo, a schedule with responsibilities identified, or a budget and expect everyone to respond without further direction. This day-to-day direction is part of the job of project manager.

4.3. Produce Results

The individual activities are performed as scheduled by the persons and organizations responsible, and budgeted moneys are spent to produce the end items or deliverables.

Each activity in a project is really a microproject itself. Activities individually meet the definition of a project: Each activity has a definite statement of work, a definite start condition or date, a required duration or completion time, and an expected level of quality. The project manager must constantly ensure that all the activities are identified and someone is assigned to perform each.

4.4. Accommodate Change Requests

The goal when planning is to predict and control the future. Nevertheless, unforeseen events do occur.

Planning is never perfect—things will change, better ways of doing tasks will evolve, and problems will arise—so the project must be sufficiently flexible to accommodate change.

A process for approving and accommodating changes in an orderly fashion is essential for all projects. Large projects have "configuration management" personnel and formal "change boards." Smaller projects require the project manager and an administrative assistant, if one is available, to perform the same functions.

As project manager, you are also the leader. Members of the team will look to you to initiate changes, even though you might expect a particular item to be within their area of technical expertise or responsibility.

Changes involve rework of previously completed paperwork—statements of work must be updated, budgets changed, schedules changed, performance requirements updated, and corrections made where errors occurred. This takes effort on the project manager's part to make sure changes are reviewed, approved, or rejected and then introduced into the formal paperwork and processes of the project.

Step 5. Communicate and Coordinate the Work

5.1. Coordinate work.
5.2. Prepare progress reports.
5.3. Hold project reviews.

Step 5 is very closely related to Step 4; in fact, it usually is initiated in conjunction with Step 4.3 and performed in parallel. It is important to communicate with stakeholders. Two important methods of accomplishing this are through progress reports and project reviews, which are sufficiently important to break out as specific steps in the methodology. Stakeholders are interested very simply because they are involved in the outcome of the project. The project manager must ensure this is a collegial relationship and not an adversarial one.

Many of the substeps of Steps 5 and 6 consist of items that could be defined in a communications plan (e.g., formats of progress reports). Individual organizations using this methodology may choose to combine these items and develop templates as appropriate.

5.1. Coordinate Work

The project manager cannot just send out pieces of paper and expect things to happen the way he or she envisions. Some people recommend "management by walking around," but others think of this as snooping. There are many books on leadership and human relations. It is extremely important to communicate with the persons supporting your project to make sure that they are aware of their responsibilities and to give them an opportunity to discuss their successes and problems. Many managers use weekly staff meetings for this purpose.

In structured project teams established as "teams-of-peers" with crisply defined roles and responsibilities, the project manager exercises leadership by facilitating conflict resolution. (See Part 4.4, Communications, for a further discussion of this important topic.)

> The trick is not only to make sure that the team members are communicating with you, the project manager, but also that they are communicating with other members with whom they have interdependent work activities.

5.2. Prepare Progress Reports

Preparing and delivering progress reports is an important aspect of the project manager's job. It is important to keep stakeholders apprised of progress and problems (especially the project manager's supervisor and the project sponsor or customer). It is important for customers and sponsors not to be surprised when project problems occur that need their help resolving. Some warning always should have been provided. It also is important for stakeholders to read the reports and provide timely and constructive feedback to the project manager. Within each parent organization, it is useful to have a standard format for all project managers to use when providing progress reports to senior management.

Figure 2.32 depicts an abbreviated and edited list of the data the Department of Defense and other departments require in the monthly progress reports for some larger projects.[33] Many projects use a variation of these items tailored to their specific conditions. (A Department of Homeland Security RFP issued in early 2005 referenced this data item description.)

As you can see, the reporting requirements may be extensive. On the other hand, these are all items the project manager should be monitoring. The progress report also provides an ongoing historical record of the progress, so it is incumbent on the project manager to make sure it is complete and accurate, especially in its description of progress and identification of problems and proposed solutions. Most construction projects require photographs to be taken at frequent intervals to document progress and justify progress payments.

Figure 2.32. Sample Monthly Progress Report Contents

SUMMARY—Brief statement of overall project status covering progress and problems. Include impact and recommended solutions to problems.

1. STATUS
   a. A statement as to whether or not the program/project/activity is on schedule; if it is not, the effort planned to meet the schedule shall be indicated. Include an overall status of each milestone, activity, or unit of work. Include updated schedule sheets, milestone charts, or activity synopsis sheets identifying phase of activity and percentage of completion of each activity, technical instruction, or order.
   b. A comparison of achieved end-product performance capabilities projected against contract baseline values, requirements, or allocations.
   c. Effort expended on each task to date, and a brief description of technical developments and accomplishments.
   d. Key dates in any testing program and a description of tests performed and significant test results.
   e. A list of all designs completed and a brief description of each item. For designs in process, provide estimated dates for design and drawing completion.
   f. A narrative of outstanding problems existing as of the previous status report and their resolution status.

continues

Figure 2.32. Sample Monthly Progress Report Contents (continued)

---

g. New problem areas encountered or anticipated, their effect on the overall work effort/project, and steps being taken to remedy problem situations.

h. Significant results of conferences, trips, or directives from the contracting officer's representatives.

i. Any other information that may cause significant changes in the program schedule.

2. FUTURE PLANS
Summary of future plans, recommendations, and proposals, both for the next reporting period and for any long-term plans.

3. ITEMIZED PERSON-HOURS AND COSTS
Itemized person-hour and cost expenditures incurred for the reporting period and cumulative by WBS, task, and cost category, total contractual expenditures, and funds remaining as of the reporting date.

4. CONTRACT DELIVERIES STATUS
The status of each deliverable end item, including data deliveries, as required by the contract. Provide item and contract identification, shipping/transmittal data, acceptance status, security classification, and scheduled due date information.

5. REPORT PREPARER
Names of persons preparing the report and their telephone numbers.

5.3. Hold Project Reviews

Project reviews should be held regularly for two reasons: (1) to give the customer and sponsor an opportunity for face-to-face dialog with the project manager and, if feasible, the project team and (2) to allow the project team to get feedback regarding the direction of the project and the progress of current or proposed work. Reviews also help morale and motivation when higher-level managers show interest in the work going on in the project. The frequency of these reviews will depend on the size and duration of the project. Monthly reviews are common. Alternatively, one or more in-process reviews (IPRs) may be scheduled at key intervals.

Project reviews tend to be more formal than other internal project meetings because they include both the customer and sponsor and may include senior management and contractors. The focus is on performance as measured against the SOW, meeting the purpose and intent of the project, and cost and schedule performance compared to the baselines. They generally follow a typical agenda, such as that shown in Figure 2.33.

Figure 2.33. Project Review Agenda

I. Introductions
II. Opening statement
   * Purpose, length of meeting, responsibilities
III. Discussion
   * Technical performance
   * Schedule status
   * Budget status
   * Labor hour status
   * Contractor progress
   * Review of open action items
IV. Conclusions/assignments
   * Summary of new action items
V. Next meeting date and location

One customer uses a small software package programmed in dBase to keep track of the action items coming from each monthly project review. Each action item is described, along with the action officer, due date, status, and WBS number.

Project reviews and meetings are both excellent forums for the project manager to review status and problems, initiate corrective action, and coordinate project policy and philosophy. The information addressed at the project review is similar to that included in progress reports.

A fixed agenda should be established for project reviews to ensure that the important information is presented and that trends can be identified. Accountability is important.

One project manager working for a government organization changed his part of the agenda at every project review given to senior management and focused on interesting general subjects. The purpose was to avoid revealing many of the existing problems and thereby to avoid accountability.

If project managers are not holding project reviews, senior managers should require them so that they can mentor and assist the project manager in the discipline of managing the project, show they are interested in the project, and help solve problems.

D. CONTROLLING STAGE

Forty years ago, Dr. Earnest Dale wrote:

> The modern concept of control envisages a system that not only provides a historical record of what happened to the business as a whole but pinpoints the reason why it happened, and provides data that enable the chief executive or the department head to take corrective steps if he finds he is on the wrong track. Also, it enables managers to identify trends—in costs, in markets, in all matters of the business—and so affords a guide for future action.[34]

Dr. Dale notes that this concept was included in writings of one of the directors of the Peninsular & Oriental Steam Navigation Company in 1875, who was unhappy with reports he was receiving from the bookkeepers and was describing what he needed and why.

The process of project control is not very complex or sophisticated. In fact, it is deceptively simple:

1. Collect data on actual performance

2. Compare this actual data to the plan

3. Identify significant variances or trends

4. Analyze the impact on project objectives

5. Initiate corrective actions

6. Replan as necessary.

All that is needed, therefore, is the ability to collect the data, a plan to compare it to (see Steps 3.7 and 4.1), and a person responsible for correcting the problem.

Step 6. Track Actual Performance

> 6.1. Identify data and data sources/develop data collection systems.
> 6.2. Collect and record the data.

Collection of time, cost, and performance data for the scheduled activities and resources is performed in Step 6. The project management methodology focuses on identifying performance metrics that relate to the output of the project in addition to traditional measures.

6.1. Identify Data and Data Sources/Develop Data Collection Systems
In many organizations with higher levels of project management maturity, the data sources and data collection systems are standard, operational, and effective. If the organization is very low on the project management maturity scale, however, the project manager may have to design and implement these internal management systems. Data on actual performance are required to compare to the plans.

The five aspects of data collection are:

1. Identify *what* data are required

2. Identify *where* or *who* the data will come from

3. Identify *how* you will get the data

4. Identify *when* you will get the data

5. Determine the *format* of the data.

This list suggests two obvious problems: (1) there may not be any mechanism in place to collect the data or (2) the existing mechanisms may not collect data that are comparable or relatable to the project plans.

6.1.1. What Data Are Required?

Controlling schedules, cost (resources), and performance is necessary when managing projects effectively. The project must be completed at a specific time for a predetermined amount of resources, and the end products must meet performance or quality criteria.

There are two categories of data: (1) planning data that are based on estimates that comprise the project schedule and cost (budget) baselines and (2) "actual" data that represent the actual measured performance achieved when work on specific activities is being performed. Schedule data need to be collected on the specific dates that activities were started and completed: cost data, including the actual number of hours each person spent working on each activity or work package and the actual nonlabor cost expenditures, and actual performance to be compared to specifications or quantitative requirements. The schedule data must be collected for each activity. The number of hours each person actually spent is collected for each activity, work package, summary WBS element, or project, depending on the level of control required on the project. Performance data are collected based on the required performance of the deliverable items and the tasks described in the SOW.

Actual data collected as the project work proceeds from week to week typically include:

• Person-hours of labor spent per activity, work package, or project

• Direct costs spent per activity, work package, or project

• Actual start and completion dates for activities and milestones

• Actual quality or performance measures, (results of testing or other metrics).

From a management perspective, it is important to recognize the difference between measuring input and measuring output. Too often managers use input measures alone as surrogates for progress.

The government inspectors at a port of entry were reporting how many inspection hours were spent that month; they then used that figure to show that they were improving food safety—just because they were spending more hours. There was no measure of the actual numbers of items inspected and accepted or rejected, nor of the planned number of items.

One of the principles of earned value (discussed in Appendix B) is to relate the expenditure of resources to the value of actual work accomplished as measured by the originally budgeted value of the work package. Just because you have spent money does not necessarily mean that you have performed any useful work.

The first two items in the list above measure input to a project, not output. The data become much more meaningful when activities are completed and not just being worked on. However, these are useful data when compared to the planned expenditures and analyzed in comparison to work actually completed. The actual activity start and completion dates relate to output because something was accomplished, and it is easy to tell if it took longer than planned. Most quality and performance data metrics also measure output.

Experienced project managers tell many stories about how activities become reported as 90 percent complete, but that the last 10 percent takes more time than the first 90 percent.

Control is achieved by comparing actual progress to plans and taking action when variances occur; therefore, the required data must be comparable to the data included in the plans. It is assumed the plans and the work authorizations can be compared to each other and have similar units of measure, hours, dollars, dates, elapsed time, etc. For schedule control, schedule data are required; for cost control, cost data are required. If you plan and authorize work by person-hours, then you must collect person-hour data.

On small projects, detailed resource planning is usually performed during the proposal preparation phase to arrive at the estimated cost (Scenario 4). Once the contract is awarded (Scenario 2 or 5), the people working on the project are assigned personal budgets in terms of the hours available for their effort. They report actual hours and costs expended on a periodic basis to the project manager, and control is exercised at the total project level or at the SOW task level.

It appears obvious, but the data required also need to relate to the costs for which the project manager is responsible. An accounting system that can provide cost data only by department and not by project is not very useful. The cost data also need to relate to the cost reporting and invoicing requirements of the project. In Part 3, Scenario 5, the project manager is paid through the customer's accounting system, and customers usually set requirements for the type and format of the data to be submitted with the invoice. None of this is really very complex; however, it does mean you might have to talk to the accounting, finance, or administrative personnel in your organization to ensure that the correct data are collected and are available when needed.

One category of costs we have ignored so far in this step is indirect costs. These costs are important to the overall management of private sector projects where a contract exists and total costs must be recovered. The project manager rarely has any control over indirect or overhead costs; therefore, identifying and collecting these data are normally the purview of the organization's accounting and financial management. The project manager must understand what these costs are and how they affect the project. (For a more complete discussion, see Step 3.4.)

> In cost-type contracts, planned overhead rates are provisional. Future overhead rates depend on the projected level of business activity (i.e., backlog). When a company does not achieve the expected level, the overhead rates increase because overhead expenditures tend to stay constant or be "sticky" regarding downward movement; accordingly, the base gets smaller. This causes problems for both the contractor and the customer.

6.1.2. Where Will the Data Come From?

Data come from a few limited sources: schedule data come from the persons working on the individual activities, resource data (the number of person hours spent on an activity, work package, or contract) usually come from the person directly, and cost data come from the accounting system. Labor hours may be entered onto timesheets and from there entered into the accounting system, or they may be recorded into the accounting system directly.

In project management the important metric is labor hours spent because this is easily understood and budgeted and translates directly into labor costs. It is also necessary to manage "direct costs." These are defined simply as those costs other than direct labor that are charged to the project and for which the project manager is responsible.

"Direct costs" include such items as travel, the cost of material and supplies, consultant costs, telephone costs, shipping costs, computer purchases, and any other similar items. These must be planned and authorized the same as labor costs.

If data are to come from the accounting system, there must be a mechanism for collecting them from the source, relating them to the appropriate work element of the project, and entering them into the accounting system. (As noted, on small projects, sometimes the only identification regarding work breakdown is to the top-level project name.) All cost data related to the project must be coded so that they can be identified to that project. All cost data also must be coded so that the organization incurring the cost is identified, as well as when the cost was incurred. Finally, the cost category needs to be identified (e.g., travel, material, telephone).

Within an organization, the various pieces of paper that authorize the expenditure of monies or resources usually include the project reference and a "charge number." When monies are expended, the appropriate charge number (account number) is entered into the accounting system, along with the amount.

Now you know why the administrative officer gets upset about late submittal of travel vouchers. Think about it: If you are working on a contract, the company cannot submit an invoice containing the cost of the trip until approximately the end of the month in which you submit an approved voucher. The project manager does not have any information on the cost of your trip from the accounting system until then. Then payment occurs approximately 30 days after the customer receives the invoice. On smaller projects, the cost of travel can be a large percentage of the total costs incurred, and the persons worrying about project costs may not be getting timely data.

Accounting systems are designed to help management run the company and not necessarily to help the project managers. In smaller companies in particular, or in companies with few projects, the accounting system may not be capable of easily collecting and segregating costs by project, WBS element and activity, category, and organization except by setting up special codes. The number of digits required for an account in the accounting system also can get very large.

Labor data usually come directly from the persons working on the project and are recorded in the accounting system. Financial reports are phased to paydays. When a paycheck is prepared, a long delay occurs between when the labor hours were actually expended and when they appear in a project cost or labor report. This delay makes them minimally useful for managing project labor costs.

For this reason, many organizations use timecards or timesheets that are submitted weekly, and project reports track labor hours on a more realistic time scale for project management. Many project managers use these data as an early check on progress. These do not have the accuracy of the accounting system, because the internal checks and balances are not performed until later in the accounting cycle, but they are sufficiently accurate for most project management situations.

Figure 2.34 presents a sample form used to collect person-hour resource data on a weekly basis; it also provides a large amount of related data useful to the project manager. This is the data collection form that one organization uses for IT projects; it is actually is a combination data form and progress report. It focuses on person-hours of labor and actual start and completion dates. This approach works well in government organizations and other organizations where it is not feasible to use other time-keeping mechanisms.

In many white-collar companies, the use of timesheets is common. Each person identifies the projects, tasks, and activities worked on each day and the number of hours. Included are overhead accounts and provisions for sick and leave time. These timesheets vary in complexity and sophistication.

Figure 2.34. State Department of Revenue Team Member Progress Report

To:	Adam Soles	Report Period Ending:	
From:			
Project Name:	PTA Mainframe Migration Development	Agency:	DOR/ISP

Concerns or Issues with tasks I worked on this reporting period are:

Issues:

Description	Date Identified	Impact	

Scheduled Vacation/Training:

Description	Start Date	End Date

continues

Figure 2.34. State Department of Revenue Team Member Progress Report (continued)

Time Reporting by Activity

Task WBS/ ID	Schedule Status	Hours to Date	Hours this Week	Estimate to Complete
	Reporting Period Total			

6.1.3. How Will You Get the Data?

You need to plan how you will get the required data. Data do not normally just appear.

In one Baltimore company, each project had a master schedule that included the interfaces among organizations as well as the planned time spans for major work items. Every Friday the schedulers from each functional organization would meet with the planners working for the project managers, and they would report actual and expected completions of all current activities, including any potential slippages.

Data need to travel from the source to the project office. Once it has been determined what data are needed, it is necessary to verify that they will be provided to the project office on a routine basis. Ways of transmitting or communicating data include:

- Reporting at a regular scheduling meeting

- Using e-mail

- Using intracompany mail

- Using an accounting system report

- Using an intranet

- Entering data into an online project management system.

Regardless of the mechanism, the project manager must verify that the data will be delivered reliably on an agreed-upon schedule.

6.1.4. When Will You Get the Data?

The frequency of the data collection and subsequent input into a project database depends on the data element and the collection procedures used. It is customary for schedule data to be reported weekly; person-hour data to be reported weekly or biweekly, depending on the payroll cycle and the pace of the project; and direct cost data to be reported at the end of the first or second week of the next month after the costs were incurred.

Accounting systems are normally on monthly cycles. Even that varies, though, depending on the payroll system. If personnel are always paid on a Friday, the accounting system may be based on closing the month on a Friday. In each quarter, one "accounting month" can be five weeks long. Although this difference of one extra week per quarter seems small, it could affect interpretation of the monthly cost reports.

To *control* a project, the project manager does not need accounting system accuracy. Timeliness is more important. The project manager is comparing actual expenditures against plan. When the accuracy of the plans is considered, it becomes apparent that the project manager does not need accounting data that are accurate to the penny. An accurate accounting system is essential for managing and accounting for funds but not for day-to-day project management.

6.1.5. What Should Be the Format of the Data?

The format of the data should enable the project manager to compare the actual performance data against the plans. Schedule and cost status format often is determined by the requirements of the project management software and the format chosen for the input data.

The format is important to make it easier on the project manager to identify variances and also to establish an audit trail. The internal procedures and directives should specify the formats. They are standardized in an organization considering the environment and culture as well as the basic project management needs.

When negotiating or planning the data collection system, make sure the format is convenient and useful for the project manager as well as the persons reporting the data.

6.2. Collect and Record the Data

The final step in this sequence is to collect and record the data. The process and media will depend on the activities of Step 6.1, and the preferred media for recording the data is project management software. Because schedule and cost baselines usually are established and controlled using this software, the software makes it easy to perform the activities of Step 7.

Data can be input directly into the software from one or more of the sources listed in Step 6.1.3 or by keyboard from written material or forms.

Performance data are normally collected manually from various devices that measure product performance and are then recorded in reports that provide the basis for further actions, if needed.

Test reports, quality control reports, and the like are used. For service projects, the data may be in the form of questionnaires filled out by the persons using or involved in the delivered services. For results projects, data are collected on the performance of the final result. IT projects are similar to products in the way their data are collected and recorded because specific tests are performed and recorded documenting the IT system's performance.

Step 7. Analyze Project Progress

7.1. Determine variances from the baseline and determine trends.
7.2. Perform analyses and determine the need for corrective action.

Control is the determination of progress toward objectives according to the predetermined plan. Any gap between expectation and performance—on the part of the entire company or any segment of it—is most easily closed if it is detected before it becomes serious.

The seventh major step involves comparing actual time, cost, and performance data to the baselines or the standards. Project management software greatly facilitates this process for schedule and cost management. The analysis identifies which variances are significant and what caused them. Finally, it is necessary to determine what if any corrective action is required. Step 8 discusses methods of initiating corrective action.

The processes of Steps 7, 8, and 9 are also identical to the process of risk management in Part 5.3, except that they are based on identifying variances from the control system rather than independent analyses. Significant variances may result in the processes of risk management also being used.

7.1. Determine Variances from the Baseline and Determine Trends

To perform this step, there must be a baseline (Step 3.6) and there must be valid and complete actual cost or schedule data (Step 6.2). During Step 3, variance limits should have been identified for the critical checkpoints and other key performance parameters and included in the project plan (and also in the charter prepared in Step 1). The data collected should be recorded in a time-scaled form so that trends can be determined. Data that should be collected for selected WBS elements include resources, costs, earned value, cost variances, and schedule variances. Experience and risk analyses are used to determine appropriate data to monitor for trends. Project management software can support this task.

There are two variance values of interest: (1) the current variance determined by comparing the actual data to the plan at the time the data were collected and (2) the projected impact of the variance on key project events or critical control points. An example of the former is the overrun or underrun of the cost of a work package. An example of the latter is the impact of all the variances on the total project budget. The former case is simply a picture of a point in time; in the latter, the picture is put into perspective. (This is actually similar to the risk assessment process described in Part 5.3.)

For schedule data, it is customary to monitor the critical path. The current variance is the actual duration of an activity compared to the scheduled duration, and the trend is determined by keeping records of the change in the value of slack or float in the critical path or at critical milestones.

Measuring trends in performance other than schedule or cost is difficult but not impossible, and the capability needs to be built into the project plan. Without such forethought, if the final product is a report, for example, the quality of the report either in content or presentation may not be known until it is drafted and the customer reviews the product. Checkpoints can be included in the schedule and project reviews held to discuss the contents. The project plan can address what will be included in the report and what data will be collected and analyzed; there will be sufficient warnings to correct any problems before the final product is completed.

In areas other than cost and schedule, the project manager may have to develop performance metrics to fit the uniqueness of the project and identify trends early.

7.2. Perform Analyses and Determine the Need for Corrective Action

Criteria developed in the planning step can assist in determining when parts of the project are out of control. An out-of-control condition arises when the variance or trend exceeds predetermined limits. Most variances will be minor and may require only an awareness that they exist and communication of the situation to another affected organization or person.

Variances do not automatically indicate poor performance. The problem may be that the plan was overly optimistic or otherwise inadequate, or that other unanticipated constraints or considerations affected performance. Experienced organizations will have performed a good risk assessment that will provide guidance in setting variances. Cumulative variances may indicate an adverse trend that needs to be corrected. An analysis of project data must be performed and the results documented. Often the customer or sponsor requires this in progress reports; however, it is good practice to document project progress at regular intervals in one form or another.

Mechanically determining the acceptable limits of a particular variance is rarely possible. The analyst's judgment is important. Of most interest are the projected impact of variances on the overall project cost and schedule and the performance of the deliverable items. Advanced techniques such as earned value readily provide information on such impacts on cost and schedule. Another advanced technique, critical chain project management, also includes algorithms for identifying the significance of variances. (See Appendix B.)

Status and variance information, as well as the results of analyses, must be communicated to the project manager or other people on the project if the project manager is not directly performing the analyses. The analyst needs to have the experience or the tools to determine when corrective action is necessary. This step is completed when specific variances that require action are identified.

Step 8. Initiate Corrective Action

    8.1. Identify action item and action officer.
    8.2. Facilitate the corrective action process.
    8.3. Arrive at a resolution.

Step 8 is one of the project manager's important direct leadership responsibilities. It is urgent to bring the process back under control when variances exceed allowable limits or adverse trends exist. If variances exceed allowable limits, corrective action is necessary whether the variances are positive or negative. A significant cost underrun in a WBS element or an exceptionally early completion of an activity or series of activities may require action to take advantage of the situation.

8.1. Identify Action Item and Action Officer

The first step in initiating corrective action is to identify the action item clearly. Many projects use the equivalent of an "action item log," as discussed in Step 5.2. This can be a spreadsheet, database, or simple table listing the item requiring corrective action and the person responsible. Figure 2.35 shows a typical format of an action item list. Sometimes a column is added to identify where the action item came from, such as "Project Review on March 3." On larger projects, the number field may include the WBS element as a prefix. This table is often laid out in horizontally and may be printed on legal-size paper.

Figure 2.35. Action Item Status List

No.	ACTION ITEM	RESP	DUE DATE	DATE COMPLETE	NOTES
1.					
2.					
Etc.					

It is important to identify the person who will take responsibility for correcting or recommending an appropriate corrective action to resolve the problem. The person may be the project manager or another member of the project team. The action is preferably delegated to the person responsible for the functional area of the project where the action is required.

Corrective action may be initiated by providing direction at a project review, by memorandum, or by other means depending on the project's characteristics and its environment. Major problems sometimes justify establishing a "Tiger Team" to solve the problem and implement the solution. It is important to remember that the person responsible must correct or address the action item specifically identified and report on its status at each project review.

8.2. Facilitate the Corrective Action Process

The project manager must assist the person responsible for taking corrective action and provide guidance concerning timing and possible alternatives. The project manager must assure the team that corrective action is being taken in a timely manner to resolve problems early, demonstrating that he or she cares about correcting problems quickly so that they do not grow larger. The same applies to senior staff, customers, and sponsors when problems are brought to them.

Many problems are resolved by modifying the project plan. Planning is not a perfect science and is a continuous process. "Work-arounds" and backup plans are normal project management mechanisms. The project manager, with the support of senior managers and sponsors, must develop an environment where the focus is not on placing blame but on developing cooperative solutions to problems to achieve project objectives.

8.2. Arrive at a Resolution

When a variance has been identified and a person has been identified to resolve the problem, the next step is to arrive at a specific resolution of the problem that the variance has identified. A significant variance demonstrates a project risk item. Just like the process of determining what to do when a risk has been identified, there are six options:[35]

1. Do nothing, and accept the variance (risk acceptance)

2. Change the baseline to eliminate the variance—change the SOW, the deliverable schedule, the budget, or the contract (risk avoidance)

3. Develop a "work-around" plan to resolve the problem and bring the overall project back under control (risk protection)

4. Obtain more information before making a decision (risk research)

5. Use existing contingencies or reserves (risk reserves)

6. Require the organization where the problem exists to make necessary adjustments (risk transfer).

All of these options are not available for each variance, especially in smaller projects. Whenever a significant variance occurs, the project manager should inform the customer or sponsor. Depending on the problem, the project manager also may inform the customer or sponsor of the solution chosen or discuss options. The natural tendency is to wait to inform the customer or sponsor until the problem is resolved. This is usually a mistake. It is especially important to notify the customer when a contract item delivery date is threatened, a cost overrun is possible, or the performance or quality of the delivered product may be reduced.

Risk management is also discussed as a facilitating element in Part 4.3.

Step 9. Incorporate Changes (Replan as Required)

9.1. Change management—baseline management.
9.2. Perform routine replanning.
9.3. Renegotiate the scope if necessary.

The activities to be performed in this step depend on the specific action determined necessary to resolve a problem or simply to take into account differing circumstances from those that existed at the start of the project.

9.1. Change Management—Baseline Management

It is normal as the project work progresses for changes to occur. These may arise from almost any source: identifying alternate methods of achieving the objectives being proposed; considering new methods of reducing risk; taking corrective action when variances exist in the project cost, schedule, or requirements; or simply improving or correcting existing plans. The project plans and schedules are predicated on certain assumptions regarding the future, such as the availability of resources and the time duration to perform activities. Problems and situations arise that require changes in plans.

A process must be in place for reviewing, approving, and implementing change requests, regardless of the source or reason for the change. Changes can affect scope, cost, schedule, product performance, or quality and may require extensive replanning. The sponsor and other stakeholders often need to be involved.

Change requests can take many forms—oral or written, direct or indirect, externally or internally initiated, and legally mandated or optional. Changes may be needed simply to correct mistakes in baseline documents, such as misspellings. Figure 2.36 presents the form used by an IT organization to request consideration of changes.

Project change control is concerned with managing actual changes as they come about. Overall change management requires processes for:

- Establishing cost, schedule, and performance baselines and defining project scope (see Step 3.6)

- Ensuring that changes are reviewed, coordinated, and approved before implementing the change, including changes to the product scope and the project scope

---

Figure 2.36. Project Change Request

1. General Information	WBS No.:
Requestor Name:	Requestor Contact Information:

Date of Request:

2. Description of Change Request

Instructions: *Provide a detailed description of the defect or requested change. If change involves a defect, indicate its frequency of occurrence.*

3. Business Justification for Change

Instructions: *Describe how the business, project, or product will benefit from this change.*

4. Effects of Not Making Change

Instructions: *Describe any effects to the business, project, or product if the change is not made.*

5. Time frame

Instructions: *Indicate desired or required time frame for addressing the proposed change.*

• Ensuring that approved changes are made to the baseline documents and the revised work plan and that information on the change is transmitted to the affected persons, organizations, and stakeholders

• Ensuring that the change management process is working.

A change control system is a collection of formal, documented procedures that define the steps by which official project documents may be changed. It includes the paperwork, tracking systems, and approval levels necessary to authorize changes. Many change control systems, especially on larger projects, include a change control board (CCB) or a material review board (MRB) responsible for reviewing change requests and making recommendations to the project manager. This board, sometimes known as a configuration control board, usually includes representation from the major organizations supporting the project. On small projects the change management function may be performed by the project manager. Regardless of "how," the function must be performed.

"Configuration management" is the term used to describe any rigorous change control system. The Department of Defense has published specifications on how configuration management systems should operate when used on its major projects.[36]

Through the change control process, updating the project plan or revising a contract may be necessary and appropriate stakeholders may need to be notified. The causes of the change should be noted in the documentation for future reference and for preparing a "lessons learned" report during the closeout phase of the project. The reasoning behind corrective actions taken to resolve significant variances should be documented for future reference.

> The bottom line is that changes will occur to every project, and the project manager needs an organized formal methodology or procedure to deal with them.

Additional discussion of configuration management is included in Section 5.6.

9.2. Perform Routine Replanning

Frequent replanning is the nature of project management, and internal operations and procedures must anticipate and accommodate this environment. Replanning is necessary when changes affect the schedules of successor work packages. Replanning is not necessary when changes occur within a work package or series of work packages because actual durations of activities vary from the schedule; they are the responsibility of a specific organization or person and do not affect succeeding work packages or activities.

Replanning associated with corrective actions may include revising the project schedules or budgets while remaining within the overall project objectives. More often than not, the replanning is driven by the need to coordinate the activities of various team members to ensure that project objectives are met. The logic network may be revised to do things differently, the project manager may use slack or float to adjust nonschedule-critical activities, "work-arounds" may be developed, or reserve or contingency funds may be used (as discussed in Step 8.3). If the information in the project plan changes, parts of Step 3—Planning, must be repeated. In all cases, the changes must be coordinated with all affected parties. This is the same process that was used at the start of the project.

Replanning that requires formal changes to the schedule baseline should go through a configuration management process.

9.3. Renegotiate the Scope if Necessary

Control is not merely seeing that people do what they are supposed to do. Management plans not only to reach certain objectives but to reach them by certain means. A good control system will indicate not only when there are deviations from the plan but also when external circumstances make it advisable to change the means of gaining the objectives or even to change the objectives themselves.[37]

It may be necessary to repeat Steps 1, 2, and 3 to correct a major variance or to accommodate a large proposed change. Whenever it is necessary to change the objectives of the project to solve a problem, it is usually necessary to revise the baseline and all related documents and plans. The customer, project sponsor, senior management, and other stakeholders all must be involved in this process.

Changing objectives could include establishing a new completion date for the project for delivery of end items, increasing project funds to cover work being added to the project, changing specifications to add or delete a feature of the end product, or changing the nature of the service provided or result expected. These are all scope changes and require changes to the baselines. There should be a formal review process to change the baseline. The project manager's charter, in addition to the project plan, also may need to be revised.

E. CLOSEOUT STAGE

When the final product is delivered, the service provided, or the result attained, is the project team's natural tendency is to have a party and move on to other work. However, the project manager must perform several important actions before the project can be completely closed out.

Step 10. Complete the Project

> 10.1. Prepare a closeout plan and schedule.
> 10.2. Get customer agreement and notify the team.
> 10.3. Archive project data.
> 10.4. Prepare a "lessons learned" document.
> 10.5. Send the customer the bill.

At the end of each project, a series of steps needs to be taken to close out the project.

10.1. Prepare a Closeout Plan and Schedule

A closeout plan and schedule (punch lists) are required for many projects. The activities performed may be to sort materials used during the project and file or store them. They also may include finding alternative assignments for project personnel. On many projects, a final audit of costs is required before final payment can be made. On construction projects, a final walk-through must be taken and a punch list completed. (This item may be part of Step 4.3.) This work must be planned, scheduled, and budgeted; this is part of the project manager's responsibilities.

If a contract is terminated before the project is completed, costs associated with the termination will need to be estimated and budgeted. Even on internal projects, commitments that have been made may need to be resolved. When contracts are terminated because of poor performance, the closeout can become very messy and expensive.

The project manager may have put together an effective team to perform the work. As the leader, this person may be expected to help the team to find other work, write recommendations, and provide awards for performance.

A few years ago, a large project was canceled "for the government's convenience" due to strong political pressure. Insufficient funds were appropriated to perform the work required in the closeout plan, and the agency was forced to return to Congress to request additional funding to close out the project. The agency actually required more money to terminate the project than to finish it, and it took several years to finally close out the project.

10.2. Get Customer Agreement and Notify the Team

There is always a deliverable item or a goal to be reached at the end of the project, and a customer or sponsor sign-off in one form or another is required. Everyone associated with the project needs to be informed that it has been completed. For projects in which cost controls are being implemented, the accounting department must be informed to stop accepting charges to the project.

10.3. Archive Project Data

Project data should be collected, sorted, indexed, and archived according to the organization's standard procedures. This can be a big job on large projects—and not very exciting. On smaller projects this step may be represented simply by a few inches in a file cabinet.

Organizations should have a process and procedure for maintaining important materials for a specific period of time. Relying on the project manager to keep a file on the project is not much help when he or she moves to a different organization. Where organizations have a person with the title "contracts manager," this person usually takes charge of archived materials.

> The same project that was terminated for the government's convenience had many file cabinets of materials worth retaining. Since this was a government project, the materials were archived in a government storage facility in Maryland. All the boxes had to include a list of the materials contained in them and be appropriately marked on the outside.

10.4. Prepare a "Lessons Learned" Document

The purpose of a "lessons learned" (or "best practices") document is to assist project managers in subsequent projects that will operate in a similar environment. The document should be prepared at a formal meeting called for the purpose of discussing the project; the meeting should be held within two weeks of final delivery of the end item. Cost data also should be collected where they can be used to help estimate the costs of similar projects in the future. Of special interest are parametric cost data relating to the organization's products.

This does not have to be a lengthy, formal document, and the purpose is not to place blame for problems that occurred.

A small company in Arlington, Virginia, routinely requires each project manager to hold a "lessons learned" meeting at the end of the project in which the team discusses what went well and what could have been done better. This is written up for the use of other project managers on new, similar projects. No names are included.

10.5. Send the Customer the Bill

When performing work under government contracts, the final closeout of the project may not occur for months or years after all work has stopped. This is likely the case on cost-type contracts. There must be a final accounting for all costs and payment of fees that may have been withheld, and overhead rates need to be audited and verified. Also, many forms need to be completed with various certifications. For products delivered with warranties, the books may not be completely closed until the warranty period expires.

Final payment under some types of contracts depends on all the work being completed, including delivery of final reports, computer CDs, a final cost audit, and all the monthly progress reports. Several minor deliverable items may be buried in the boilerplate of the contract. It is the project manager's responsibility to ensure that everything is completed to receive final payment or final sign-off of the project from the customer or the sponsor.

The vice president of projects at a Virginia IT company that sold complete systems to its customers asked the instructor of a project management training course to impress on his project managers the importance of completing their project paperwork so that they could receive payment. Getting the systems working was important, but so was completing all the contractual items, such as delivering manuals and spare parts.

REFERENCES

1. Peter F. Drucker. *Management: Tasks, Responsibilities, Practices* (New York: Harper & Row, 1974), pp. 182–183.
2. Henry Gantt. *Organizing for Work* (Easton, NY: Hive Publishing Company, 1974).
3. Lewis Carroll. *The Complete Works of Lewis Carroll* (New York: The Modern Library, Random House, 1922).
4. Michael Dobson. *The Triple Constraints in Project Management* (Vienna, VA: Management Concepts, Inc., 2004).
5. Harold Koontz and Cyril O'Donnell. *Principles of Management,* 2d ed. (New York: McGraw-Hill, 1959).
6. For a complete discussion of the WBS, see Gregory T. Haugan, *Effective Work Breakdown Structures* (Vienna; VA: Management Concepts, Inc., 2002), or Gregory T. Haugan, *The Work Breakdown Structure in Government Contracting* (Vienna; VA: Management Concepts, Inc., 2003).
7. U.S. Department of Defense. *Work Breakdown Structures* (MIL-HDBK-881, 2 January 1998), p. 4.
8. Sample WBS courtesy of J.D. Carter, Rockwell-Collins Inc. Used with permission.
9. Critical Tools, Inc. *WBS Chart Pro* (Austin TX: Critical Tools, Inc.) (www.criticaltools.com).
10. Peter S. Cole. *How to Write a Statement of Work, 5th edition* (Vienna, VA: Management Concepts, Inc., 2003).
11. Michael G. Martin. *Delivering Project Excellence with the Statement of Work* (Vienna, VA: Management Concepts, Inc., 2003).
12. Ibid., p. 80.
13. Ibid., pp. 83–87.
14. Peter S. Cole. *How to Write a Statement of Work, 5th edition* (Vienna, VA: Management Concepts, Inc., 2003), p. 153.
15. U.S. Department of Defense. *Handbook for Preparation of Statement of Work* (MIL-HDBK-245D, 3 April 1996), p. 22.
16. Ibid., p. 4.

17. Ibid., pp. 9–10.
18. Ibid., p. 4.
19. U.S. Department of Defense. *Defense and Program-Unique Specifications Format and Content* (MIL-STD-961E, 1 August 2003), pp. 4 and 6.
20. Frederick Winslow Taylor. *The Principles of Scientific Management* (New York: Harper Brothers, 1911, republished by Dover Publications, Mineola, New York, 1998), pp. 62–63.
21. Robert W. Miller. *Schedule, Cost, and Profit Control with PERT* (New York: McGraw-Hill, 1963), p. 42.
22. This is sometimes called a PERT network. This is a misnomer since "PERT" refers to a specific type of logic diagram. See Gregory T. Haugan, *Project Planning and Scheduling* (Vienna, VA: Management Concepts, Inc., 2002), p. 28.
23. The Gantt chart shown is a variation of a Gantt chart illustrated in a collection of papers titled *How Scientific Management is Applied* (Chicago, Illinois: The System Company, 1911), *Chapter II: The Five Steps to the One Best Way,* by H.L. Gantt, p. 18.
24. For the rules used to calculate the logic networks, see Gregory T. Haugan, *Project Planning and Scheduling* (Vienna, VA: Management Concepts, Inc., 2002), pp. 67–72.
25. Steve Neuendorf. *Project Measurement* (Vienna, VA: Management Concepts, Inc., 2002), p. xii.
26. U.S. Government, Office of Management and Budget. *Planning, Budgeting, Acquisition, and Management of Capital Assets,* OMB Circular No. A-11, Part 7, June 2002.
27. American National Standards Institute. *Earned Value Management Systems,* ANSI/EIA-748-1998 (Arlington, VA: Electronic Industries Alliance), approved May 19, 1998.
28. M.A. Daniels. *Principles of Configuration Management* (Rockville, MD: Advanced Applications Consultants, Inc., 1985), p. 108.
29. This section is adapted from Gregory T. Haugan, *Project Planning and Scheduling* (Vienna, VA: Management Concepts, Inc., 2003), p. 76.
30. Harold Koontz and Cyril O'Donnell. *Principles of Management,* 2d ed. (New York: McGraw-Hill, 1959).
31. Glenn M. Parker, ed. *Handbook of Best Practices for Teams* (Amherst, MA: HRD Press and Irwin Professional Publishing, 1996), Chapter 5, "The Team Formation Checklist: A New Team Activity," Zenger-Miller, Inc., p. 43.
32. Parviz F. Rad and Ginger Levin. *Achieving Project Management Success Using Virtual Teams* (Boca Raton, FL: J. Ross Publishing, 2003), p. 57.
33. U.S. Department of Defense, *Data Item Description* DI-MGT-80368, 8 June 1987.
34. Ernest Dale. *Management: Theory and Practice* (New York: McGraw-Hill, 1965), p. 482.

35. Paul S. Royer. *Project Risk Management, A Proactive Approach* (Vienna, VA: Management Concepts, Inc., 2002), p. 35.

36. U.S. Department of Defense. MIL-STD-973, *Configuration Management* (Washington, D.C.: Office of Secretary of Defense and Joint Logistics Commanders, AMSC No. D6728, 17 April 1992).

37. Ernest Dale. *Management: Theory and Practice* (New York: McGraw-Hill, 1965).

Applying the Methodology

While the standard methodology presented in Part 2 is used to manage each project, the manner in which it is implemented varies with the type of project. For example, the start-up actions of projects vary widely with the type of project. Therefore, this Part 3 includes several scenarios that in total are intended to be a complete set of the major types of projects. Each scenario represents a variation in the implementation of the methodology.

When you are assigned to or starting a new project, the approach you take, especially in the first three steps of the methodology, is determined by the conditions under which the project is established and the information that is provided or available at start-up. This part presents seven different starting conditions or scenarios, each of which requires a different approach to implementing the project management methodology and steps covered in the Part 1. These seven scenarios are:

Scenario 1. Direct Assignment from Supervisor or Sponsor—The typical project is based on a direct request from a supervisor or sponsor to perform a job, making sure specific objectives are met within cost and schedule constraints. This might involve solving an internal problem such as a division moving to a new location, establishing an advertising campaign, or performing a feasibility analysis.

Scenario 2. Direct Assignment from Another Organization—Another operating division or organization makes a request for support in solving a problem. An example may be to upgrade a database and improve the query capabilities, to develop an operating and maintenance manual for a new product, or to flight test a new glider design. In general, the supporting organization contains skills or is responsible for a function not available in the requesting organization.

Scenario 3. Project Manager—Outsourcing—Outsourcing is performed when an enterprise lacks the necessary skills or facilities in-house to perform a project or part of a project. This situation is common for many government organizations developing products or performing studies. It is also common for large private sector projects where work is subcontracted. The project involves defining the work to be outsourced, developing a request for proposals (RFP), managing the procurement process, and monitoring the performance of the contractor selected.

Scenario 4. Respond to a Solicitation—The company has received an RFP and decides to respond. The response is planned and managed as a project. This project is the first phase of being the recipient of the outsourcing from Scenario 3.

Scenario 5. Perform to a Contract—The company has been awarded a contract for a project based on responding to an RFP (Scenario 4) and now must produce.

Scenario 6. Starting a Life Cycle Program for a Product—The program manager is tasked to proceed and develop a great idea for a new product. The feasibility phase is to be completed initially and will lead into an entire program. All the life cycle phases of the program must be planned and managed.

Scenario 7. Taking Over an Ongoing Project—The current project manager has been reassigned, and a new project manager is taking over the work in the middle of the project.

All these scenarios require applying the same project management techniques and principles. However, while all the same methodological steps are required, the emphasis is different and the application will vary. This part addresses some general issues and considerations. Each of the seven different project scenarios is then presented, illustrating how the methodology is adapted and modified to meet each situation.

START-UP QUESTIONS—STEP ZERO

Figure 3.1 lists several questions that must be answered at the start of the project. The answers to many of the questions depend on the start-up conditions: How did the project come about? What was the assignment to the project manager? All the questions are not applicable to every project. The answers also are dependent on the culture and normal way of managing projects within the enterprise.

Figure 3.1. Start-Up Questions at Step 0

a. *Requirements*—What is the project? What is the product/service/result? Is the business case to be supported?

b. *Statement of Work (SOW)*—Is there an SOW? What work is to be performed?

c. *Specification*—How good does the product have to be? What level of performance is expected?

d. *Quality*—What does the customer or sponsor expect?

e. Schedule—When does the product/service/result need to be finished/delivered?

f. *Budget*—How much money will I have for the project?

g. *Resources*—Who will do the work? What help will I have?

h. *Authority*—What control do I have over my resources? How do I get it done?

i. *Mentoring*—What assistance is available from the sponsor/supervisor/enterprise management?

j. *Communications*—What internal reports are required? Reviews?

k. *Lessons Learned*—Which "lessons learned" or "best practices" documents from previous projects are relevant to this project?

l. *Customer*—What are the critical "hot buttons"?

New project managers need the answers to these questions to be able to perform their jobs effectively. The questions also represent an outline of the project management job and the perspective that is required.

Large projects often have different project managers for each phase in a project's life cycle (see Appendix C). For example, if the project involves responding to a request for proposals, the customer project manager has already determined the feasibility and gone through the initiation phase. You are immediately in the planning phase. This is the case in all except one of the scenarios: someone else has made a determination that the project is feasible or has completed the conceptual definition, and the initiation phase is completed. Exactly where the scenario is in the life cycle process is the determination made in "Step 0"—establishing the project parameters as outlined in the questions found in Figure 3.1. A person with a technical background may refer to them as "boundary conditions."

Do not forget to gather lessons learned. This is the output of previous projects from Step 10.4. What has been learned? Where are the pitfalls? What worked and what didn't work? What are the best practices that should be followed? Talk to the customer. Find out which aspects of the project and its output are most important.

APPLICATION OF THE METHODOLOGY TO THE SCENARIOS

The methodology discussed in detail in Part 2 is summarized in Figure 3.2 for reference. Each step is then discussed for each of the seven scenarios to illustrate its varying implementation depending on the different conditions under which the project manager may be taking on the project.

Figure 3.2. Methodology Steps

1. Establish the project objectives
    1.1. Develop the statement of objectives
    1.2. Define the deliverables and their requirements
    1.3. Develop the project (manager's) charter
2. Define the work
    2.1. Develop the WBS
    2.2. Prepare a SOW
    2.3. Prepare the specification
3. Plan the work
    3.1. Define activities and activity durations
    3.2. Develop a logic network and schedule
    3.3. Assign and schedule resources and costs
    3.4. Develop the cost estimate
    3.5. Establish checkpoints and performance measures
    3.6. Establish project baselines
    3.7. Develop the project plan
    3.8. Approve the project plan
4. Perform the work
    4.1. Budget and authorize the work
    4.2. Add staff resources
    4.3. Produce results
    4.4. Accommodate change requests
5. Communicate and coordinate the work
    5.1. Coordinate work
    5.2. Prepare progress reports
    5.3. Hold project reviews
6. Track actual performance
    6.1. Identify data and data sources/develop data collection systems
    6.2. Collect and record the data
7. Analyze project progress
    7.1. Determine variances from the baseline and determine trends
    7.2. Perform analyses and determine the need for corrective action
8. Initiate corrective action
    8.1. Identify action item and action officer
    8.2. Facilitate the corrective action process
    8.3. Arrive at a resolution
9. Incorporating changes (replan as required)
    9.1. Change management—baseline management
    9.2. Perform routine replanning
    9.3. Renegotiate scope if necessary
10. Complete the project
    10.1. Prepared a closeout plan and schedule
    10.2. Get customer agreement and notify the team
    10.3. Archive project data
    10.4. Prepare a "lessons learned" document
    10.5. Send the customer the bill

SCENARIO 1. DIRECT ASSIGNMENT FROM SUPERVISOR OR SPONSOR

Scenario 1. Direct Assignment from Supervisor or Sponsor— The typical project is based on a direct request from a supervisor or sponsor to perform a job, making sure that specific objectives are met within cost and schedule constraints. This might involve solving an internal problem, such as a division moving to a new location, establishing an advertising campaign, or performing a feasibility analysis.

Scenario 1, Step 0. Project Phase in the Life Cycle

The first step is to be aware of the phase of the project in the life cycle. In this scenario, the person making the assignment (a supervisor or sponsor) has already determined the feasibility. (If this is not the situation, go to Scenario 6.) That person also may have already determined a preliminary or target budget for the project and a target date by which the project is to be completed.

Scenario 1 is the most common type of project, especially in enterprises that manage by projects. The execution of each step of the basic project management methodology is discussed in the context of this scenario. The assumption is that this is a small- to medium-sized project. Large projects follow the same methodology, but the documentation is much more extensive and formal.

This first scenario is actually the basic scenario used to develop the steps of the methodology. Little tailoring is required.

Scenario 1, Step 1. Establish Project Objectives

1.1. Develop the statement of objectives.
1.2. Define the deliverables and their requirements.
1.3. Develop the project (manager's) charter.

Scenario 1, Step 1.1. Develop the Statement of Objectives

The very first step is to know where you are going: What is the project supposed to achieve? Assignments are not always clear and crisp, and often they are simply vague. The person making the assignment may not be able to express the objectives clearly for many reasons and may be leaving it up to the project manager to provide a succinct set of objectives. The project manager may be required to complete the work of the initiation phase and get clarification and agreement on the specific objectives. Preparing a written statement of objectives and reviewing it with the sponsor may provide a mechanism to clarify the objectives.

The project objectives the supervisor or sponsor initially provides to the project manager may be in writing, or they may be oral instructions. Often they are included in a memorandum to the staff notifying them of the existence of the project and identifying the responsible project manager. The objectives provide the basis for the planning phase and may or may not be completely developed. The project manager's first actions are to expand on or further clarify the objectives and to reach agreement with the supervisor as part of defining the scope of the project.

The project manager and the supervisor might want to discuss the method by which the assignment is to be announced to the rest of the organization. The method should include the key aspects of the project requirements and the project charter.

Scenario 1, Step 1.2. Define the Deliverables and Their Requirements

The requirements include the quantitative items of "what, when, where, how many, how much?" discussed in the basic methodology. The project manager and project team need a clear picture of what they are to deliver, whether a product, service, or result; the required performance or quality of the product they will deliver; and the criteria for acceptance by the customer.

Scenario 1, Step 1.3. Develop the Project (Manager's) Charter

The project charter is an important document that provides the vehicle for documenting and negotiating the answers to the questions posed in Figure 3.1 and Steps 1.1 and 1.2. The specific content of the charter must be tailored to the organization and culture where the project is located.

For the Scenario 1 project, the important areas are the description of the end product and the expected quality or performance; the availability and source of resources to perform the project, including dollars and personnel; the schedule; and reporting requirements. (Other items may also be important, depending on the environmental elements described in Part 4.)

A preliminary project manager's charter should be developed and published at the initiation of this type of project, but a complete project charter may not be able to be completed until the remainder of the planning work is completed, when it evolves into the project plan.

If extensive planning is required, the planning phase may need to be treated as a project in itself, with the output of the project being a project plan for the next phase.

Scenario 1, Step 2. Define the Work

2.1. Develop the WBS.
2.2. Prepare a SOW.
2.3. Prepare the specification.

Scenario 1, Step 2.1. Develop the WBS

A WBS is essential for all projects. The project manager needs it for identifying and organizing the work in a logical framework—to ensure that all the work is identified, planned, and scheduled. The type of WBS will vary as discussed in Part 2, Step 2.1, depending on the specific type of project: product, service, or results.

Scenario 1, Step 2.2. Prepare a SOW

The WBS provides the outline for the SOW, which also should include the specific deliverables and the delivery schedule. Since this project is being performed in-house, a minimal SOW may be all that is needed, and in some cases a written SOW may not be necessary as long as the project team understands the work to be performed and the schedule.

An easy and recommended way to prepare an SOW is to start with a WBS dictionary and add to the element descriptions.

However, it is normally useful for the project manager to prepare an SOW, if only to make sure that he or she has thought out all the work to be performed. This can also be achieved by preparing a WBS-based schedule, as discussed in Step 3.1.1.

Scenario 1, Step 2.3. Prepare the Specification

The performance of the end item or deliverable of the project is described in a specification when a discrete product is produced. A "requirements document" performs the same function for "results" projects. In this latter case it describes what the project manager expects to provide in terms of the result. An SOW describes what work will be performed, and a requirements document describes the performance expected from the deliverable item.

For results projects, the statement of objectives and the "how good" part of the project requirements will usually suffice.

Service projects, such as putting on an international conference, have as a deliverable a "successful conference," which is rather vague but typical of this category. For service projects, the SOW, including the parameters of the service, will serve as a requirements document.

Scenario 1, Step 3. Plan the Work

> 3.1. Develop activities and activity durations.
> 3.2. Develop a logic network and schedule.
> 3.3. Assign and schedule resources and costs.
> 3.4. Develop the cost estimate.
> 3.5. Establish checkpoints and performance measures.
> 3.6. Establish project baselines.
> 3.7. Develop the project plan.
> 3.8. Approve the project plan.

Scenario 1, Step 3.1. Define Activities and Activity Durations, and Step 3.2. Develop a Logic Network and Schedule

Using software such as MS Project®, the WBS should be entered in the activity field, as discussed in Step 3.1.1 and used as the framework for defining the activities. During the same process, predecessor and successor activities should be identified to generate the logic network. In addition, the person preparing the MS Project® schedule should add estimates of the costs and resources required for each activity.

A consultant or experienced staff member may be asked to estimate the resource hours and the direct cost items for each activity. These are then discussed, reviewed, and modified as necessary by the responsible personnel. This process ensures that the experience of the consultant or staff member is reflected in the estimate and that items are not inadvertently omitted. It also saves time for the responsible personnel and does not require them to be experienced with the software.

The project manager and project team should review the results of the planning using MS Project® reports and data exported to other software, such as Excel®, and repeat the planning process until satisfied with the project schedule, resource assignments, and total cost.

For a project of less than approximately 250 activities and WBS elements, the draft MS Project® schedule, if developed by the project manager, can be completed in a few hours, certainly in less than a day. The team would then review it with the project manager the next day and finish this step of the methodology within a couple of days of the start date.

Scenario 1, Step 3.3. Assign and Schedule Resources and Costs

Assigning and scheduling resources should be performed while loading data into MS Project® or the project management software. "Resources" in this case means labor resources. Depending on the software, labor resources are identified and added to each activity as hours per activity per person or skill category; the quantity of a particular resource to be assigned to the activity for the duration of the activity; or, as is often the case, the percentage of working time available for the person assigned to an activity. In any event, the software will convert these data to labor costs using a resource table or equivalent device.

The resource table identifies unit costs for the individual labor resource. Resources can be identified and added at the same time as activities or at a later pass. Resource histograms can be generated to determine if the resource loading is acceptable and adjustments made accordingly. Resource leveling can also be performed using the software, as discussed in Step 3.3 of the methodology.

If relevant, cost elements must be identified and estimated for each activity. This includes all materials, purchased equipment, travel, telephone, Internet, and the like that are chargeable to the project. This is tedious work. It takes discipline and time—but not as much as you might think. The question is often asked: "How am I to know what travel I will be doing a year from now on my project?" The answer is that if you are using a WBS for the framework and have identified all the activities to be performed within each lowest level WBS element, then you have identified all the work. If you know your business, you will know which activities require travel and to where. The rest is routine.

Your estimate is not set in concrete. You will use the project process of managing routine change, Step 9.2, to change this cost element when better or more data are available. This also is the reason to build in contingency.

> Some companies have designed forms to be used with each activity or work package that collect these estimates from the responsible manager or worker. The labor is also often spread by time on the activity, and all the cost elements are identified. Clerical labor then is used to enter these data into the project management software.

Scenario 1, Step 3.4. Develop the Cost Estimate
If the project is in a private-sector organization, its estimated total cost is a significant item of interest. If all activities are identified, and the cost of each activity estimated, then the project management software will total the activity estimates. The labor rates included in the computer must provide the type of cost you are after. As discussed in the meth-

odology, Step 3.4, overhead and G&A rates may need to be added to arrive at the total price.

Scenario 1, Step 3.5. Establish Checkpoints and Performance Measures

Checkpoints such as "in-process reviews," quarterly progress reviews, and preliminary design reviews should be established and incorporated into the schedule. Performance measures such as subsystem tests to verify the meeting of specification requirements also should be included.

On small projects, the performance measures may be simply milestones. For example, in a physical move to another facility, the milestone "All workstation items packed" may be a significant milestone and checkpoint because it implies that the boxes are ready to be picked up and moved and identifies when the moving vans need to arrive.

Performance measures: On a rewrite and reorganization of a very large manual (800+ pages) for a Department of Defense organizational element, the rewrite included the requirement to make sure it could be understood by persons of a seventh-grade education. Sample pages in each chapter were required to be subjected to review by special computer reading-level assessment software before being submitted to the client.

Scenario 1, Step 3.6. Establish Project Baselines

When the project manager, project team, and other stakeholders are in agreement, they establish a baseline schedule and budget. The baselines are necessary to provide a basis for control.

Scenario 1, Step 3.7. Develop the Project Plan

For smaller projects, the project plan can be a combination of: (1) the charter or authorizing document; (2) the SOW, if a written one is prepared; and (3) the MS Project® output, which includes resources, responsibilities, the budget, and the master schedule. The three items do not need to be bound into a separate document, as is frequently the case in larger projects.[1]

Scenario 1, Step 3.8. Approve the Project Plan

The purpose of the project plan is threefold: (1) to get necessary approvals to proceed with the implementation phase or, at a minimum, to make sure that the supervisor/sponsor supports the plan; (2) to establish a sound basis for performing the implementation activities of the project; and (3) to provide the basis for control. Even if not formally required, it is good practice to get approval from the supervisor or sponsor to proceed with implementing the plan. When presented to the supervisor or sponsor, necessary changes may be needed in terms of budget, schedule, the SOW, or perhaps even the requirements. The steps must be repeated as necessary to get to the point where approval to proceed is received and all stakeholders are on board.

Scenario 1, Steps 4–10, are the same as identified in the basic methodology, Part 2 of this book.

SCENARIO 2. DIRECT ASSIGNMENT FROM AN ORGANIZATION YOU SUPPORT

Scenario 2 addresses the situation in which one organization receives a request from another operating element of an organization to provide support. An example is an IT project to upgrade its database and improve the query capabilities, to develop an operating and maintenance manual for a new product, or to flight test a new glider design. In general, the receiving organization contains skills or is responsible for a function that is not available in the requesting organization. This scenario is presented from the point of view of the organization receiving the request for support.

Scenario 2, Step 0. Project Phase in the Life Cycle

The typical support project is similar to the project discussed in Scenario 1, except that there is normally a much more formal interface between the project manager and the sponsor because they are usually from different organizations within the organization, and the sponsoring organization may be providing funding. In some organizations, the sponsoring or requesting organization also is permitted the option to outsource the support to offset the monopoly position of the supporting organization. Managing an outsourced project is the subject of Scenario 3.

The sponsor in Scenario 2 is from another part of the project manager's organization and typically has a problem to be solved or a performance enhancement or some other outcome that will produce a beneficial change within the organization. IT projects are typical of Scenario 2. As shown in the life cycle for IT projects in Appendix D, the sponsor has already determined the desirability and is ready to move on to getting the project started. The sponsor already may have determined a preliminary or target budget for the project and a desired schedule. Or it may be a two-step proposal process, with the prospective project manager first providing a cost estimate and proposed schedule to the sponsor, negotiating them and the work statement, and then proceeding with the project.

The estimated cost and completion date may force the sponsor to reevaluate the project or the assumptions. The result may be a quite different project with significant changes in the statement of work.

For that to be accomplished, however, the first three major steps of the methodology should be completed. The actual implementation of the project will follow the generic methodology of Steps 4–10.

The methodology for Scenario 2 differs from that of Scenario 1 primarily in Step 1, establish the project objectives, and the three substeps. The remaining steps are the same as in Scenario 1.

Scenario 2, Step 1. Establish Project Objectives

> 1.1. Develop the statement of objectives.
> 1.2. Define the deliverables and their requirements.
> 1.3. Develop the project (manager's) charter.

Scenario 2, Step 1.1. Statement of Objectives, and Step 1.2. Define the Deliverables and Their Requirements

Steps 1.1 and 1.2 are often combined in this scenario. The sponsor from the operating organization or the organization requiring assistance provides the objectives, deliverables, and requirements the deliverables must meet to the project manager. They should be in writing and include the budget and schedule or expected completion date. In some organizations in which this is a normal activity, a standard "request for support" form or a project authorization form is used that incorporates elements from the project charter described in Part 2, Step 1.3. The resulting document is an internal contract and authorization to expend resources and proceed with the work.

Often, working out the objectives, deliverables, requirements, budget, and schedule is an iterative process in which the sponsor and project manager jointly develop the project and its parameters. This iteration is in essence a planning phase used to clarify and define the requirements of the overall project.

The succeeding steps are the same as those in Scenario 1. Appendix D includes some additional items for IT projects.

SCENARIO 3. PROJECT MANAGER—OUTSOURCING

Outsourcing is performed when an enterprise lacks the necessary skills or facilities in-house. This is the normal situation for many government organizations developing products and for large private sector projects for which work is subcontracted. The project involves defining the work to be outsourced, developing a request for proposals, managing the procurement process, and monitoring performance of the contractor selected.

Many organizations outsource work through contract or subcontract. A project manager of such a project—the one who does the contracting out—applies the project management methodology with a different perspective than the project manager who is actually performing the work.

The contracting out of project work deserves an entire book to itself. Two such books are those by Engelbeck, which focuses on U.S. government acquisition practices (or "how to do it if you work for the U.S. government") and Huston, which addresses managing project procurement activities (see Bibliography). This book focuses on the basics and does not get involved in the quasi-legal intricacies of procurement and contracting practices.

To eliminate confusion in this Scenario 3, the organization that is actually outsourcing the work is referred to as the "customer," and the organization seeking and eventually being awarded the work is referred to as the "contractor."

Scenario 3, Step 0. Project Phase in the Life Cycle

For work to be outsourced or contracted out, the customer must plan sufficiently to define the desired work and to solicit proposals from experienced and effective organizations.

Some market research may be required to verify that there are qualified organizations to do the required work. The U.S. government has it relatively easy: It is able to place a "Sources Sought" notice on the Federal Business Opportunities website, and potential contractors will respond with a description of their qualifications.

To procure work, the customer must complete the initiation phase as well as much of the planning phase. The project life-cycle phases overlap, as illustrated in Figure 3.3. The contractor performs the initiation phase effort and enough of the planning phase to be able to issue an RFP. The RFP in effect is a partial project plan, but it is presented in a format that will facilitate the submittal of proposals by prospective contractors and the subsequent selection process. The RFP includes additional information that would not be in a project plan. (See Part 4, Project Procurement Management. Also review Scenario 4, Responding to an RFP, to see the guidance provided to an organization responding to an RFP. This will provide additional insight into the proper way to prepare an RFP so that good, responsive proposals will be submitted.)

Figure 3.3. Scenario 3 Life-Cycle Relationships

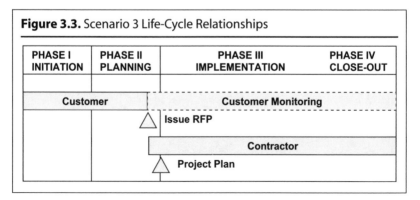

PHASE I INITIATION	PHASE II PLANNING	PHASE III IMPLEMENTATION	PHASE IV CLOSE-OUT

When intending to contract out work, the customer's effort consists of two parts: (1) a project covering the initiation phase and part of the planning phase, with the final product being an RFP; and (2) a process of monitoring the performance of the successful bidder.

Scenario 3, Step 1. Establish Project Objectives

1.1. Develop the statement of objectives.
1.2. Define the deliverables and their requirements.
1.3. Develop the project (manager's) charter.

Scenario 3, Step 1.1. Develop the Statement of Objectives
The project objectives are defined in the same manner as in the generic methodology and provide the basis for the specific requirements the deliverables must meet. These requirements are included in the solicitation or RFP, which will be advertised and sent to prospective bidders. These are also developed similar to the process outlined in Scenario 2.

In some acquisition activities of the U.S. government, especially since 1996, the RFP may include a comprehensive statement of objectives (SOO). This is intended to eliminate a detailed SOW from the RFP (Step 2.2) and put the responsibility for the SOW on the organizations responding to the RFP.[2]

In this scenario, the government SOO includes more background information and information on the objectives and purpose of the solicitation than normally would be in an objective statement that was complemented by an SOW. This approach requires the prospective contractor to define the contract WBS, the SOW tasks, and sometimes the delivery schedule for the primary items.[3] For government SOOs, the website that provides a source of acquisition information is www.acqnet.gov/Library/OFPP/BestPractices/pbsc/home .html. A link goes to the "Seven Step Guide to Performance-

Based Services Acquisition." Within the steps is the description of how to create and use an SOO.

Scenario 3, Step 1.2. Define the Deliverables and Their Requirements

The project manager intending to outsource the work must define the deliverables, whether product, service, or result. This includes not only the products to be delivered, but any data such as progress reports, manuals, and draft and final reports. For service projects, the primary deliverable may be defined in terms of the objectives to be achieved. Even for service projects, there are normally data products such as progress reports and final reports to be delivered; these must be identified and defined.

The Department of Defense has tried to bring order to the submittal of data on a contract. The typical RFP includes a standard attachment called a contract data requirements list (CDRL) that has information on each data deliverable, including "when, where, how many?" and other information, such as the related SOW paragraph. The CDRL entry also refers to a data item description (DID), which specifies in detail the contents of the data item itself. DIDs are available on the Internet.

> RFPs that use the comprehensive SOO approach and no SOW also request that the prospective contractor propose appropriate CDRL items in addition to some core items that may be in the RFP.

Scenario 3, Step 1.3. Develop the Project (Manager's) Charter

A complete project manager's charter might not be needed in this scenario because managing outsourced projects is often a normal part of the person's job description, and the actual size of the project of getting the RFP out the door is relatively small. However, if performing the source selection process or managing the resulting contract requires additional resources not readily available, the charter becomes important.

On larger contracts, the project manager may need contractor support to assist in preparing the solicitation or managing the contract. However, if some guidelines are provided by the project sponsor (who may also be the project manager's supervisor) or a program manager, a partial charter may be required. This is especially the case if the guidelines include an overall budget, the delivery dates of the end items, the expected performance, or any combination. The sponsor may be the organization that is to use the deliverables from the project in its operational activities. The charter provides a mechanism to make sure that the project manager and the sponsor are communicating on what specifically is to be outsourced and how the process of acquisition and management is to be performed.

Scenario 3, Step 2. Define the Work

2.1. Develop the WBS.
2.2. Develop the SOW.
2.3. Prepare the specification.

The WBS, SOW, and product specification (or some similar document defining performance of the end item, whether product, service, or result) are all developed as discussed in the generic methodology. However, there are some very important considerations when outsourcing.

Scenario 3, Step 2.1. Develop the WBS, and Step 2.2. Develop the SOW
These two steps often are performed simultaneously or in an iterative process.

The WBS is the outline of the SOW. The SOW, like the WBS, often is more complex than appears on the surface, especially when used as part of a solicitation or contract.[4] Although having an outline before you begin to write is preferable, many people do not use outlines and are more comfortable drafting the SOW from scratch or modifying an existing SOW. This is definitely not the recommended approach. If the SOW is drafted without an outline or a WBS, be sure to analyze the after-the-fact outline of the SOW to make sure it meets all the requirements of an effective WBS. (See Part 2, Step 2.1.)

There are four principal reasons it is so important to have a harmonized WBS and SOW: (1) it helps ensure that all the work to be outsourced is identified and described, including the bidder's project management activities; (2) the project control mechanisms will be more effective; (3) it provides a framework for submittal of the cost estimates that facilitates analysis; and (4) it provides a framework for effective communication between the buyer and seller. Remember, once the contract is signed, it may get very expensive to make changes if items were inadvertently omitted or it may not be possible to collect desired data if the contract SOW is structured badly. Contractors like to "get well" on changes.

> If the project manager wants certain items to be accomplished, performed, or delivered after a contract is awarded, they must be identified in the RFP and included in the contract.

Scenario 3, Step 2.3. Prepare the Specification

Preparing a product specification is more complex than it appears on the surface and is usually performed by the technical personnel supporting the project. If the project manager is the subject matter expert, he or she may have to prepare it. Obviously, this is a key document to provide to the prospective bidders because it defines the performance of the product being purchased or outsourced. In the specification, the SOW, or some other part of the contract, there must be a description of how the performance will be verified; what tests, measurements, or inspections must be performed; and where and how these tests, measurements, or inspections will be performed. Some organizations have a contract requirement that the selected contractor prepare a test, inspection, or QA plan and submit it to the customer for approval.

Scenario 3, Step 3. Schedule Work, Resources, and Costs

3.1. Define activities and activity durations.
3.2. Develop a logic network and schedule.
3.3. Assign and schedule resources and costs.
3.4. Develop the cost estimate.
3.5. Establish checkpoints and performance measures.
3.6. Establish project baselines.
3.7. Develop a project plan (RFP).
3.8. Approve the project plan (RFP).

Scenario 3, Step 3 details still address the activities of the customer.

Scenario 3, Step 3.1. Define Activities and Activity Durations
Because the work is going to be outsourced, activities must be defined and activity durations estimated only to the extent that a set of key milestones can be identified and the delivery dates of the end items established, if needed. The customer may have a date by which the project must be completed to meet some internal requirement. Milestones are needed for one or more of the following reasons:

1. To identify important delivery dates to meet operational requirements

2. To establish key performance monitoring points and key meetings or reviews

3. To identify when data and other secondary deliverable items should be submitted

4. To identify availability or timing of customer-provided facilities, items, or resources required for contract performance

5. To identify payment milestones for progress payments (if applicable)

6. To coordinate schedules at key interface points with other project or program participants.[7]

Figure 3.4 illustrates a top-level schedule provided to bidders on a GSA furniture contract to assist in planning their work.

External requirements or constraints resulting from other stakeholder activities must be identified to provide necessary planning information to the bidders. (These data are provided in the bidding documents described in Step "D" of the procurement management process in the facilitating element discussion in Part 4.5.)

Scenario 3, Step 3.2. Develop a Logic Network and Schedule, and Step 3.3. Assign and Schedule Resources and Costs

To provide schedule information for the prospective contractors in the RFP, some effort is required to develop a top-level schedule. The methodology should be followed at the most detailed level possible, recognizing that there may be minimal information available to the customer regarding certain details of the project. The schedule in the RFP needs to be realistic.

Step 3.3 is not normally performed in Scenario 3; however, there must be a baseline schedule and cost estimate. On larger projects, a schedule may need to be prepared to assist the customer in planning and scheduling the resources needed to manage the project. Steps 3.2 and 3.3 then also apply to this effort.

Figure 3.4. Master Schedule

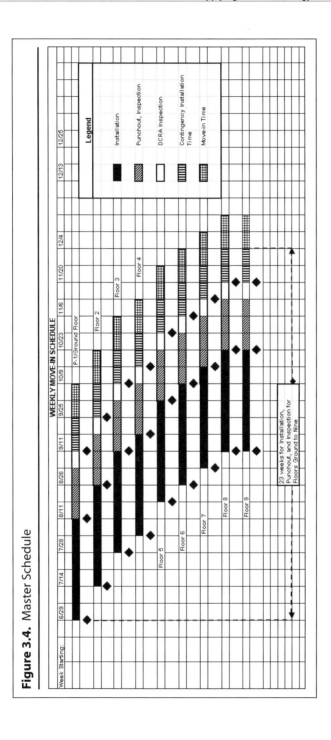

Scenario 3, Step 3.4. Develop the Cost Estimate

The customer must prepare a cost estimate independent from that submitted by the prospective contractors. A cost estimate is needed as a basis for evaluating the contractor submittals and negotiating a contract, as well as to ensure that sufficient funds are available to sign the contracts and that the timing is appropriate. The cost estimate is not normally included in the RFP.

Scenario 3, Step 3.5. Establish Checkpoints and Performance Measures

Checkpoints such as in-progress reviews and design reviews should be established in the RFP; including them in the schedule development process of Step 3.2 helps ensure that the timing is reasonable. The schedule itself is not expected to be placed into the RFP—only the key milestones.

Scenario 3, Step 3.6. Establish Project Baselines

Baselines are established to provide a basis for control. The result of performing Steps 3.1–3.5 is to provide the customer a baseline for planning and to evaluate contractor submittals.

Scenario 3, Step 3.7. Develop the Project Plan (RFP), and Step 3.8. Approve the Project Plan (RFP)

In Scenario 3, the RFP is the equivalent document to the project plan in the other scenarios or in the generic methodology. It is a partial project plan, with the addition of items needed for an RFP, such as instructions for preparing a proposal.

The U.S. government has a standard format for RFPs that also has been copied by many U.S. companies and by foreign governments. This standard U.S. format is illustrated and discussed in Part 4, Project Procurement Management. Sections A–G in the outline in Figure 4.9 and the contract attachments are the corresponding items to the project plan.

The remainder is needed for the procurement process and the contract. Note that many parts of the complete project plan, as illustrated in Figure 2.30 in Part 2, are not required for the RFP—they are to be prepared by the contractor. Once approved, the RFP is issued. Scenario 4 addresses the preparation of the response to an RFP.

At this point in the methodology for Scenario 3, the winning contractor is selected. The following sections of this scenario still are presented from the point of view of the customer, but the role has changed to one of monitoring, as illustrated in Figure 3.3.

Scenario 3, Step 4. Perform the Work

4.1. Budget and authorize the work.
4.2. Add staff resources.
4.3. Produce results.
4.4. Accommodate change requests.

After contract award, the contractor will perform the work on the project according to the contract and should follow the methodology outlined. The general job of the customer project manager is to:

- Monitor the efforts of the contractor to ensure that the work is progressing satisfactorily

- Facilitate the resolution of any problems the contractor may have

- Perform review and inspection duties effectively and professionally to avoid unduly delaying the project

- Communicate regularly and frequently with the contractor project manager to resolve problems and interpret the statement of work where ambiguities exist

- Respond to requests for contract changes.

In Scenario 3, the methodology of Step 4 does not generally apply to the customer. However, the customer project manager has ongoing duties to ensure that funds are available, to respond promptly to requests for changes, and to perform the customer tasks and obligations described in the contract. The customer must perform their responsibilities promptly and consistently.

Scenario 3, Step 5. Communicate and Coordinate the Work

> 5.1. Coordinate work.
> 5.2. Prepare progress reports.
> 5.3. Hold project reviews.

Scenario 3, Step 5.1. Coordinate Work

The customer project manager is responsible for assisting the contractor in areas in which the contractor's work interfaces with other organizations. Assistance may involve providing interface drawings, setting up meetings, making phone calls, or any of myriad activities, depending on the nature of the project and the contractual relationship.

The customer project manager must be available to answer questions. He or she must have a working relationship with the contractor and maintain open communications to facilitate problem solving.

Scenario 3, Step 5.2. Prepare Progress Reports

The customer project manager has a dual role in preparing progress reports. Like all managers, he or she has a responsibility to keep supervisors, sponsors, and stakeholders apprised of the project's status. This is important to ensure that someone higher in the chain of command does not unwittingly make a decision that adversely affects the project. Also, the project manager may need assistance in solving problems.

The genesis of the second role as a recipient of progress reports is in specifying the requirement for progress reports in the SOW or in the contract data submittals. The contents, format, and frequency also should have been defined. Is the report to be oral? Written? Monthly? Quarterly? At a minimum, the following items should appear in the progress report submitted to the customer:

1. Summary of the work performed in the reporting period

2. Descriptions of any problems and proposed solutions

3. Description of the work to be performed in the next period

4. Schedule status and trends

5. Cost status and trends

6. Actions required of the customer

7. Important decisions.

Many other items can be specified depending on the nature of the project and the risk; for example, status by task or by WBS element, test and quality control results, risk management status, meetings held, and lessons learned. The progress report also provides a historical record of project status and performance.

Scenario 3, Step 5.3. Hold Project Reviews
It is important to hold project reviews, as discussed in the generic methodology. The customer project manager is responsible for seeing that project reviews are held, that the agenda is followed, and that action items are identified and resolved. This is part of the discipline necessary to manage a project successfully.

Scenario 3, Step 6. Track Actual Performance

6.1. Identify data and data sources.
6.2. Collect and record the data.

Scenario 3, Step 6.1. Identify Data and Data Sources, and Step 6.2. Collect and Record the Data

The contractor submits project data according to the contract. The customer project manager should be maintaining a record of trends. Depending on the source of the funding, the customer's focus should be on cash flow to meet payment of invoices and the estimated costs at completion.

A customer occasionally may request the contractor to maintain a running estimate of termination costs in case the funding for the project is stopped or for any other reason that is not the responsibility of the contractor. Termination costs may be very high depending on the contract terms.

Scenario 3, Step 7. Analyze Project Progress

7.1. Determine variances from the baseline and determine trends.
7.2. Perform analyses and determine the need for corrective action.

Scenario 3, Step 7.1. Determine Variances from the Baseline and Determine Trends, and Step 7.2. Perform Analyses and Determine the Need for Corrective Action

The customer project manager needs to perform both of these steps using contractor data. The contractor may be performing both steps and reporting to the customer regularly, but the customer must be looking at the data independently and objectively to be assured that corrective action is initiated when warranted. The goal of the analyses is to determine if the actual work performed matches the reported schedule and cost data and to identify problems while there are still time and resources to initiate corrective action.

The analyses provide the basis for questions to be asked at project reviews and at other meetings to ensure that proper actions are being taken. It is normal human behavior for contractors to underplay problems and assure the customer that everything is under control. It is important for the customer to make sure this is the situation—preferably, not in an adversarial manner. A good management control system makes this process easier because the data are available to facilitate communication. Baselining concepts and risk management tools facilitate the process. In larger projects in which the use of earned value is justified, the reports facilitate performance management.

Scenario 3, Step 8. Initiate Corrective Action

8.1. Identify the action item and action officer.
8.2. Facilitate the corrective action process.
8.3. Arrive at a resolution.

Scenario 3, Step 8.1. Identify the Action Item and Action Officer

A small but important step is to make sure there is a person responsible for resolving each problem. This is a normal entry onto an "action item" list compiled at a project review or project meeting. Do not assume that just because a problem is identified, someone will assume responsibility for solving it. Also make sure the person is aware that he or she has the responsibility. Again, just because someone's name is put next to an action item and he or she is e-mailed the minutes of a meeting, do not assume that the person is aware of the assignment.

Scenario 3, Step 8.2. Facilitate the Corrective Action Process, and Step 8.3. Arrive at a Resolution

The customer project manager must take whatever action is warranted to assist in resolving problems. That is part of the job. It is true that the customer is paying the contractor to do the work, but it also is true that it is the customer's project as well. Both must work together.

Scenario 3, Step 9. Incorporate Changes (Replan as Required)

9.1. Change management—baseline management.
9.2. Perform routine replanning.
9.3. Renegotiate scope if necessary.

Scenario 3, Step 9.1. Change Management—Baseline Management
The work of planning a project involves forecasting and trying to influence the future. The tools that are available to develop schedules and estimate costs are very good when implemented properly. However, some changes are inevitable, and the customer project manager must expect the contractor to propose or submit them. Just as the contractor needs a configuration management process, the customer must have a process as well. The customer's process is one of reviewing and approving, rejecting, or modifying proposed contractor changes. This must be done quickly and efficiently so as to not delay the project.

Changes submitted to the customer usually require a change to the contract and have an impact on cost, schedule, or performance. When approved, they require a formal change to the performance baselines. The contract usually performs the work, and the customer signs off on it. The customer must have sufficient resources available to review and negotiate changes in a timely manner. This may involve the customer's contract manager (if such a person exists in the organization), the technical support staff, the finance and budget personnel, and the organization that will be using the end product.

Scenario 3, Step 9.2. Perform Routine Replanning
Routine replanning often is necessary to adjust for weaknesses in the original schedule or to update performance specifi-

cations or documents that have already been submitted. The customer must have the staff capabilities to accommodate routine replanning.

Scenario 3, Step 9.3. Renegotiate the Scope if Necessary

When trying to solve problems, especially where there is a very tight overall project cost budget, the only solution may be to modify the scope of the project—to delete or modify work or to modify the objectives. For this to be accomplished effectively, the previous steps, especially in the planning phase, must have been performed so baselines are well-defined. Repeating many, if not all, of the Steps 1–3 efforts may be necessary to redefine the project.

The customer and the contractor must work closely to make the necessary modifications to the contract and related documents.

Scenario 3, Step 10. Complete the Project

10.1. Prepare a closeout plan and schedule.
10.2. Get customer agreement and notify the team.
10.3. Archive project data.
10.4. Prepare a "lessons learned" document.
10.5. Send the customer the bill.

Steps 3–9 are largely efforts of the contractor that are monitored by the customer. Step 10 still requires much contractor effort, but this is where responsibility for the end product reverts to the customer.

Scenario 3, Step 10.1. Prepare a Closeout Plan and Schedule

The contractor is expected to prepare a closeout plan (which may be a checklist or "punch list") and schedule. The plan or list addresses all the final activities necessary to complete the contract and the deliverable items. This is normally closely coordinated with the customer because agreement is necessary on the items to be accomplished before closing out the contract.

Scenario 3, Step 10.2. Get Customer Agreement and Notify the Team

The customer project manager must be prepared to accept the final deliverable items of the contract and presumably be provided information in the contract regarding how delivery is to be accomplished, as well as what inspection, if any, must be performed. (This is discussed in more detail in the generic Step 10.2.)

Scenario 3, Step 10.3. Archive Project Data

The customer project manager must archive important project data as a historical record and have a basis for audit if necessary.

Scenario 3, Step 10.4. Prepare a "Lessons Learned" Document

This step is strongly recommended for the contractor. It is also useful for the customer project manager to provide guidance for other customer organizations in the future.

Scenario 3, Step 10.5. Send the Customer the Bill

The customer must pay for the work performed according to the contract. (The generic Step 10.5 discusses the issues involved.) The biggest problem for the customer, depending on the organization and the type of contract, is performing the final audit so that the contract can be closed out and any final payments made.

When the customer is the government, the final audit or review may take several months to complete because it is not normally performed by the   project manager's organization. So any "hold-backs" are not paid for several months until the audit is complete. Also, on cost-type contracts there may be extensive negotiations regarding which costs are "allowable" and which are not before final payment is made.

SCENARIO 4. RESPOND TO A SOLICITATION

In Scenario 3 the focus was on the work necessary to prepare the solicitation or RFP and the customer's effort to manage the project. Scenario 4 has the project manager on the other side of the table—responding to a solicitation. Scenario 5 is the next step: What do you do when you win the contract?

Companies get new business by responding to solicitations and assigning a project (proposal) manager to prepare the response. The effort of preparing a response to an RFP is in itself a project. The output of this type of project is a document or set of documents referred to as the "proposal."

Scenario 4, Step 0. Project Phase in the Life Cycle

The initiation phase, including the project justification and business case, is performed by the customer. The justification requires planning to provide the basis for a work statement, cost estimate, and schedule. This is normal for the customer project manager to get the approvals and funding to solicit bids, or to outsource work and to develop the solicitation materials. So, the customer performs part of the normal output from the planning phase and includes it in the RFP; the work of the responding proposal or project manager is to complete the planning to the degree specified in the RFP. (In many situations, a proposal manager assists the project manager in preparing the proposal.)

Scenario 4, therefore, starts in the midplanning phase of the life cycle.

Figure 3.5 presents three rules for preparing a successful proposal. These are not part of the project management methodology, but they are provided to assist a new project manager.

Figure 3.5. Rules for a Successful Proposal

There are three rules to follow when preparing a successful proposal, in order of importance:

1. *Provide the data and information exactly as requested in the RFP.* The RFP is issued by the customer, so give the customer what they ask for. RFPs from U.S. government organizations have a standard RFP format, and Sections L and M usually contain the information on what needs to be submitted and how.[5] In other venues, the customer always tells the bidders what they want in one place or another in the proposal.

2. *Provide a better proposal than your competition.* There are many dimensions to this that may include the product performance, the presentation, the price or other considerations depending on the RFP, customer, solution, etc. You always need to look for a special feature or capability to give your proposal an edge. Be different and innovative. Highlight your difference in the proposal.

3. *Work hard to make the proposal as good and as high quality as possible.* Be thorough and timely—no errors, omissions, or shortcuts in meeting Rule 1.

Scenario 4, Step 1. Establish Project Objectives

1.1. Develop the statement of objectives.
1.2. Define the deliverables and their requirements.
1.3. Develop the project (manager's) charter.

Scenario 4, Step 1.1. Develop the Statement of Objectives

The RFP defines the requirements of the project and describes its background to assist the bidder in understanding the project. The customer project manager performs this step of the methodology as it applies to outsourcing the project.

The proposal manager's objective is usually very clear: Using assigned bid and proposal funds and resources, prepare a winning proposal that is fully responsive to the RFP.

Scenario 4, Step 1.2. Define the Deliverables and Their Requirements
The customer also defines Step 1.2 for the product, service, or result being outsourced. The deliverables—in the form of the proposal itself—are also defined by the customer and included in the RFP in a section on what is required to be submitted in the proposal. (See Step 2.2 for how to use these data.)

Scenario 4, Step 1.3. Develop the Project (Manager's) Charter
The role of the charter in the generic methodology is that of a contract between the sponsor or supervisor and the project manager. In this scenario, the charter or equivalent document is also required and needs to identify the resources assigned or available to the project or proposal manager. It is no different from any other project except that the time period is usually relatively short—30–45 calendar days for many proposals.[6]

Company V had a support organization that looked like it was going to overrun its assigned bid and proposal budget. Because the Board of Directors had allocated a fixed overall budget, no additional funds were available. The organization did not finish its section of the proposal and quit work, leaving it to the proposal manager to complete the section. Company V was unsuccessful in its bid, and one of the reasons the customer gave was that the uncompleted section was deemed "nonresponsive" to the RFP. The first rule was clearly violated, with disastrous results.

Scenario 4, Step 2. Define the Work

2.1. Develop the WBS.
2.2. Prepare a SOW.
2.3. Prepare the specification.

Scenario 4, Step 2.1. Develop the WBS

The WBS is used to structure the work needed to prepare the proposal; it normally is clearly defined in the RFP, although it is not identified as such. The WBS is in the form of specific directions regarding the sections to be included in the proposal and how they should be organized. This provides the basis for identifying the persons to be responsible for preparing each section and a completion date for each section and each draft.

Another WBS is needed for the work to be performed on the project after contract award. An RFP will include either a SOW or a statement of objectives. In most other project scenarios, the WBS is developed first based on the requirements and deliverables; then the SOW is prepared. However, when responding to an RFP, the process is reversed. The reason is simple: following Rule 1 in Figure 3.5, the customer has provided the WBS directly or indirectly.

It is important to give the person issuing the RFP what they want, or Rule 1. Therefore, assume that the customer had a WBS and developed the statement of work from the WBS as the generic methodology directs.

However poorly organized the SOW is, you should nevertheless base the WBS on it as provided.

Do not assume the customer does not understand the problem or is inept just because you think the RFP could have been written better. You do not know the internal environment of the customer and therefore, cannot understand the problems. Assume the customer is competent and work with what is given. After contract award there will be an opportunity to discuss differences, resolve them, and suggest alternatives.

Two of the reasons to develop a WBS for the project work are: (1) to be able to prepare a structured master schedule that covers all the work and (2) to be able to prepare a comprehensive cost estimate that relates to the work (Steps 3.1 and 3.4 of the generic methodology). These are important steps in responding to the RFP.

Scenario 4, Step 2.2. Prepare a SOW

A formal SOW usually is not needed to prepare the proposal. However, if your organization hires consultants to assist in preparing the proposal, an SOW will be required for the consultant's contract. The consultant will prepare another SOW for the work the proposal team will perform, considering the proposal preparation itself as a project. This latter statement of work is prepared using the methodology outlined in Figure 3.6.

Figure 3.6. Proposal Organization Methodology

Following Rule 1 of preparing a successful proposal, the proposal manager should use the following approach to organize the proposal preparation activity:

a. Review the RFP in detail (emphasize "detail") and prepare an outline (WBS) of the proposal that addresses *every* item in the RFP that needs to be submitted or is necessary to support the submittal. (Also review carefully the fine print and the "boilerplate" material in the RFP.)

b. Make sure the outline is directly responsive to any instructions regarding the proposal's structure.

c. If no instructions are provided, and if there is a section in the RFP that identifies the evaluation factors, make sure the outline matches the evaluation factors. The purpose is twofold: to make sure the important items are addressed and to make it easy on the evaluators to find the relevant material in your proposal.

d. Cut and paste the specific proposal content statements into each item in the outline and describe in detail what is needed in each section, specifically.

e. Assign persons or organizations to prepare each section.

Step "d" in Figure 3.6 results in an equivalent statement of work for the preparation of the proposal.[7]

It is also necessary to focus on the SOW for the project work being proposed.

It may appear confusing, but there are projects within projects. The reason for having a Step 0 in the methodology is to orient the reader from the life-cycle perspective, where there may be projects within projects within programs.

The set of tasks in an SOW do not always include all the elements needed to make sure that all work is covered by the WBS, so add elements as necessary to ensure that your schedule and cost estimate are complete. One WBS element that must frequently be added is "project management."

Over the past several years some organizations have followed a somewhat different approach toward the SOW. Customer preparation of a WBS and SOW places responsibility for the definition of the work on the customer. The contractor may satisfactorily complete all the work described in the SOW and yet the project goals are not attained or not attained fully.

Using the philosophy that the contractor is the expert in knowing what work needs to be performed and is in the best position to define and organize the work, the RFP contains an SOO rather than an SOW (as discussed in Scenario 3, Step 1.1). It also may not contain a delivery schedule. It is left up to the contractor to submit a complete SOW with the proposal and also to propose a delivery schedule. This has two advantages for the customer: (1) it will clearly show which of the bidding contractors best understands the work to be performed to achieve the objectives, and (2) it reduces the chances that a company that has excellent proposal writers will win with an inferior product or solution.

On the other hand, if the SOO is at all ambiguous, it may be subject to wide interpretations of the work needed and complicate the evaluation process. Also, there may be very good reasons for establishing firm delivery dates in an RFP and for providing a detailed SOW.

In any event, if an RFP contains an SOO and not an SOW, it is even more important that the project management methodology, Steps 1–3, be followed carefully to prepare a successful proposal.

Scenario 4, Step 2.3. Prepare the Specification

A product specification or performance specification is normally included in an RFP when the primary deliverable is a product. A frequent requirement of the RFP is to address each line in the specification and describe how it will be met or show verification, such as test data, that the required performance is feasible. Sometimes a "compliance matrix" is requested, which is an array of each line in the specification with a column identifying whether the proposed solution meets or exceeds each item.

For the other types of projects, such as service, result, or a hybrid of the two, criteria that the end item must meet for the project to be successful—or for the contractor to get paid—must be specified. These criteria become the equivalent of the product or performance specification.

Scenario 4, Step 3. Plan the Work

3.1. Define activities and activity duration.
3.2. Develop a logic network and schedule.
3.3. Assign and schedule resources and costs.
3.4. Develop the cost estimate.
3.5. Establish checkpoints and performance measures.
3.6. Establish project baselines.
3.7. Develop a project plan.
3.8. Approve the project plan.

Scenario 4, Step 3.1. Define Activities and Activity Durations, and Step 3.2.
Develop a Logic Network and Schedule
These two steps are performed simultaneously, as illustrated
in the generic methodology. Some will argue that preparing
a detailed schedule for the project during the proposal phase
is too difficult: "How can we develop a detail proposal for
a development program when we are not sure what work
needs to be done?" Or you can substitute the word "research"
and make the same argument. The counterargument is that
you are planning the steps (activities) you will be taking during the development. If you do not know your technical
approach and the steps in the process, you should not be
bidding. Nevertheless, the planning and scheduling must
accomplished with as much detail as possible to provide a
solid basis for pricing.

As a competitive strategy, one company with good
project planning talent prepares and submits detailed
schedules with the proposal, even if not required until
after contract award. This demonstrates an understanding of the work and often impresses prospective
customers.

The two different approaches to providing SOWs in RFPs
also apply to schedules for delivery of the primary end
items. Most RFPs provide a delivery schedule in terms of
days/weeks/months after contract award; those that provide
an SOO also leave the delivery dates up to the contractor.
Like price, this then becomes an important variable to be
evaluated.

When a fixed delivery date for the primary (or all deliverables) is given, activity definition and preparation of the
logic network are performed with a different perspective.
The first step, of course, is to enter the WBS into the project
management software, and the second step is to enter all the
deliverables, data included, as fixed milestones. (Sometimes
the RFP also specifies important performance milestones

[e.g., the critical design review] to be held within six months after contract award.)

Within this framework, all the activities are defined and linked to cover all the work necessary to develop the deliverables, including the data and any performance milestones. The activity durations are established as necessary to meet the delivery requirements, recognizing that high risk may be involved in certain activity durations. The cost of performing some activities is determined by the quantity of resources necessary to perform the activity in the required time period.

Scenario 4, Step 3.3. Assign and Schedule Resources and Costs

The process of assigning and scheduling resources and costs is almost identical to the comparable step in the generic methodology, with an important difference: In the generic methodology, the goal is to match the resources to the work to come up with a resource plan to use for implementing the project. In the proposal, the goal is to use the process to come up with a cost estimate.

From the perspective of detailed planning and control, it is preferable that the labor hours and cost elements be identified for each activity; that ensures that all costs are identified. This takes considerable work and is usually performed by organizations with more mature project management systems. Cost estimating often is performed at summary WBS levels.

The sponsor and the project manager often work together to establish a schedule, price, and SOW for the project. There are more constraints in responding to an RFP, and it may take several iterations until the schedule requirements, activities, and resources are compatible. There also is the further issue of cost competition and the need to propose a competitive price.

Scenario 4, Step 3.4. Develop the Cost Estimate

The goals in developing the cost estimate, in addition to having a winning price, are: (1) to be able to provide cost data in the form necessary to meet the requirements in the RFP, (2) to develop a reasonable resource plan as part of preparing the cost estimate and price to be submitted, (3) to provide a proposal cost breakdown that will facilitate contract negotiations, and (4) to provide a proposal cost and resource breakdown that can readily be converted into a resource plan and budgets to implement the contract after award.

The biggest difficulty is the first item. RFPs frequently ask for cost data that are not readily available as standard reports from current project management software. This is especially the case when you must present the cost build-up from labor hours to final price showing overhead and G&A rates and fee.

Figure 3.7 illustrates one simple format frequently requested, and Figures 3.8 and 3.9 illustrate two of the supporting tables. Figure 3.8 illustrates the breakdown of labor hours by skill and by activity and Figure 3.9 illustrates the breakdown of the travel estimate. All these tables are prepared in a spreadsheet. (On a recent procurement, the customer provided a comprehensive Excel® model in the RFP similar to Figures 3.7, 3.8, and 3.9 and requested that the bidders add WBS and task structure, resources, costs, and labor and overhead rates in the appropriate cells.) In this case the tasks are major SOW tasks, not detailed activities. Note how the detail tables support the data in the cost proposal.

When estimated labor or cost data must be provided on a time scale, it usually is necessary to prepare the estimate at the detailed activity level and use the PM software to prepare the data. All this is not as complicated as it sounds if the methodology has been followed.

Figure 3.7. Typical Price Calculations (Standard Form)

February 22, 200X   **COMPANY COST PROPOSAL**
PROJECT ZYX

DIRECT LABOR

	HOURLY RATE	ESTIMATED HOURS	ESTIMATED COST
PROJECT DIRECTOR	$60.00	140	$8,400.00
TECHNICAL DIRECTOR	$60.00	300	$18,000.00
SYSTEMS ANALYST	$50.00	1040	$52,000.00
DATA BASE ADMIN	$30.00	520	$15,600.00
CLERICAL	$20.00	640	$12,800.00
TOTAL DIRECT LABOR			$106,800.00

FRINGE BENEFITS: 35.00%   of TOTAL DIRECT LABOR (TDL) $37,380.00
                        LABOR SUBTOTAL $144,180.00

LABOR OVERHEAD   15.00%   of TDL PLUS FRINGE $21,627.00
                     TOTAL LABOR COSTS $165,807.00

OTHER DIRECT COSTS (ODC)

	TELEPHONE/ FAX /INTERNET	$200.00
	MATERIAL AND SUPPLIES	$100.00
		$0.00
	TOTAL ODC	$300.00

CONSULTANT COSTS $0.00

TRAVEL   **$12,668.25**
             SUBTOTAL: LABOR, ODC & TRAVEL $178,775.25

GENERAL AND ADMINISTRATIVE
             9.00%   of SUBTOTAL $16,089.77

             TOTAL COST $194,865.02

FEE
             8.00% $15,589.20

             TOTAL PRICE $210,454.22

Figure 3.8. Supporting Data (Labor Hours by Activity)

| | Labor Hours | | | |
| | Task 1 | Task 2 | Task 3 | Task 4 |
				Total
Project Director	20	40	40	40	140
Technical Director	80	160	40	20	300
Systems Analyst	320	320	80	320	1040
Database Admin	40	80	80	320	520
Clerical	160	160	160	160	640
Total	620	760	400	860	2640

Figure 3.9. Supporting Data (Travel)

TRIP ONE—Data Collection
Airfare—Round-Trip—RIC—SEA	$1,750.00	
Per Diem—10 Days—$150 Lodging, $60 M&IE	$2,100.00	10 days
Local Travel—To/From Home to RIC	$112.50	
Car Rental	$500.00	10 days

TRIP TWO—Data Collection
Airfare—Round-Trip—RIC—SEA	$1,750.00	
Per Diem—5 Days—$150 Lodging, $60 M&IE— Seattle	$1,050.00	5 Days
Local Travel—To/From Home to RIC	$112.50	
Car Rental	$250.00	5 Days

TRIP THREE—Atlantic City Technical Meeting
Airfare—Round-Trip—RIC—ATL CITY	$500.00	
Per Diem—2 Days—$140 Lodging, $60 M&IE— Atlantic City	$2,800.00	2 Days
Local Travel—To/From Home to RIC and Parking	$96.25	
Car Rental	$120.00	2 Days

TRIPS FOUR AND FIVE—Project Meetings in DC
POV Home to DC	$195.00	260 miles RT
Per Diem 6 days total—$150 lodging, $60 M&IE	$1,260.00	
Parking	$72.00	

TOTAL TRAVEL	$12,668.25	

To be able to provide the data requested and be assured of its validity, it is important to follow the PM methodology. Once this is automated—that is, the activities, activity durations, and resources are loaded into the software and the spreadsheet model is complete—management review and modification of the estimate can be readily accomplished and changes made and reevaluated. Once this has been performed for one proposal, future proposals are much easier.

Scenario 4, Step 3.5. Establish Checkpoints and Performance Measures

This step is used in the proposal preparation project to identify when drafts are to be reviewed and by whom. It is common to use a "red team" to review the completed draft to make sure it is responsive to the RFP. The role of the red team is to review critically the draft proposal from the perspective of the customer. Red team members should not have participated in preparing the proposal.

RFPs frequently identify checkpoints or milestones to be included in the master schedule of the work to be performed on the project being outsourced. There is a list of deliverables that includes several types of documents, such as progress reports, test plans and results, analysis results, and maintenance manuals. The RFP also may require special management reviews or inspections.

At the same time the WBS is being entered into the project management software, these data elements, meetings, and milestones all must be input as milestones in the schedule and the work necessary to produce them must be included under the appropriate WBS element.

Scenario 4, Step 3.6. Establish Project Baselines

The proposal project manager usually establishes the schedule for preparing the proposal a few hours after the RFP is received and has been analyzed for any unusual items. Some companies have a "bid/no-bid" committee that reviews all relevant RFPs, decides which to pursue, and establishes the budget. Proposals are expensive to prepare and take resources away from other work.

> In a recent RFP, the proposal was required to be submitted with working prototypes of the items being proposed. The customer was to accomplish the testing to make sure that certain key performance parameters could be met. Then, if they passed this go/no-go step, the written proposals were opened. This was a very expensive proposal that required extensive planning.

Once the schedule for the work to be outsourced is completed using appropriate project management software, it can be reviewed and then used as a basis for any work plan that needs to be described in the proposal. Although the methodology refers to a "baseline schedule and budget," the goal in this scenario is to arrive at a workable schedule and a winning cost proposal. (After contract award, the perspective changes and budgets need to be negotiated with supporting persons and organizations.)

Scenario 4, Step 3.7. Develop a Project Plan
The project plan for preparing the proposal is discussed in Step 2.2.

A proposal submitted in response to an RFP usually includes and goes beyond the basic project plan, as described in the generic Step 3.7, because of the technical and management detail that is often required. However, it actually is a preliminary plan that has been submitted, because it is common for a milestone or deliverable in the RFP to be a formal project plan that is to be submitted shortly after contract award. This enables the customer to discuss the contents with the contractor and to make important changes. It also enables additional items, such as a complete risk analysis, to be performed and included if required.

If the basic methodology has been followed, it usually is a simple task to take the information in the proposal, the schedule, and the resource plan and update it to reflect any changes that occur as a result of contract negotiations or redirection after contract award.

As a matter of strategy in accordance with proposal Rule 2, one company routinely submitted a very detailed project plan with their proposals unless there was a page limitation. Most companies, like students, do little more than the minimum required, and this company was successful on several bids because they could illustrate their understanding of the job and readiness to proceed by presenting this level of detail.

Scenario 4, Step 3.8. Approve the Project Plan
Step 3.8 in the methodology has two components: (1) the internal review of the proposal prior to submittal, and (2) more importantly, the customer's acceptance of the proposal. Experience has shown that when the cost and schedule data in the proposal are prepared following this methodology—and the contract negotiation is related to actual work to be performed—the costs and schedule progress rapidly and smoothly because the needed data are available and credible.

SCENARIO 5. PERFORM TO A CONTRACT

The company was awarded a contract for a project based on responding to an RFP (Scenario 4) and now must produce.

Scenario 4 is the project for the work performed in responding to a solicitation; Scenario 5 assumes that your organization has been awarded the contract. This scenario is similar to Scenarios 1 and 2, but with some important differences at the start.

Scenario 5, Step 0. Project Phase in the Life Cycle

Contracts normally are awarded for project implementation, so the implementation phase of the life cycle is expected to be the next step. However, this is rarely the situation; the normal process is to repeat some of the planning phase steps. Following are some of the likely events that change the startup situation:

1. Parts of the RFP may have been prepared several weeks or even months before contract award because of the normal procedural steps required to issue the RFP and perform a fair evaluation of the competing proposals. As a result of the time lag or other factors, the SOW or some of the requirements may have changed.

2. During contract negotiations, changes to the SOW, pricing, terms and conditions, schedules, etc., may have been made.

3. The RFP as discussed in Scenario 3 may be knowingly based on summary or preliminary information, with the expectation that the winning organization will complete the planning phase after contract award (e.g., delivery of the project plan may be required 30 days after contract award).

All these conditions indicate that the real location of the project in the planning life cycle phase is somewhere before Step 3.8, Sponsor Review and Acceptance of the Project Plan.

Scenario 5. Step 1. Establish Project Objectives; Step 2. Define the Work; and Step 3. Plan the Work

A characteristic of projects is creating changes. The project itself creates change, and within the project change occurs continually. At the point where a contract is awarded, change to the project plan occurs.

Schedule a "kickoff meeting" to be held soon after contract award to get the input from the customer regarding changes and also to review customer expectations. It is rare that there will be no changes, and most likely the materials prepared for the proposal are not sufficiently current to use as a basis to proceed into implementation. It also is necessary to be aware of the customer's expectations and methods of problem solving and communicating. Complete as many of the steps of the Figure 3.10 checklist as possible before the kickoff meeting and finish the planning subsequent to the meeting.

Figure 3.10. Kickoff Meeting Checklist

Step A. Review the existing planning materials and the output products from the methodology Steps 1, 2, and 3 (and substeps) that were used in preparing the RFP.

Step B. Compare the existing documents to the signed contract and contract materials.

Step C. Identify output products from the generic methodology Steps 1, 2, and 3 that are currently undeveloped.

Step D. Update all existing documents, such as the SOW and master schedule, that were used to prepare the proposal.

Step E. Develop all missing items from the methodology Steps 1, 2, and 3 to be able to complete the project plan.

Companies frequently make exaggerated claims in a proposal to get an "edge" on the competition. The customer expects these items to be fulfilled during the implementation phase. They must be included in the project plan.

The purpose of this effort is to complete the methodology through Step 3.7, Develop a project plan.

When the customer approves the project plan, Step 3.8, then the project is ready to proceed into the implementation phase. Not all steps of the methodology will necessarily have to be repeated.

Figure 3.11 illustrates the process of reviewing and revising the project documents in view of having received a new contract. The review should have been ongoing during contract negotiations or while waiting for a formal announcement of contract award. Once the review is complete and the project documents—SOW, WBS, schedules, cost estimates, resource plans, etc.—are up to date and baselined, the project may proceed into Step 4 of the implementation phase, following the generic methodology.

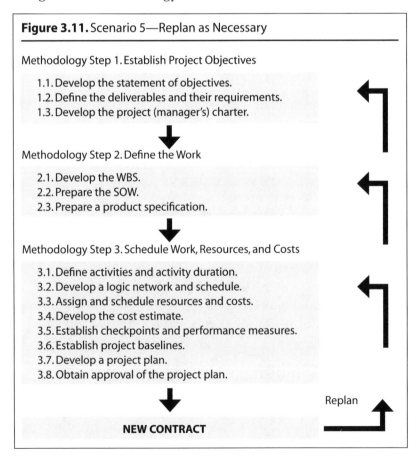

Figure 3.11. Scenario 5—Replan as Necessary

Methodology Step 1. Establish Project Objectives

   1.1. Develop the statement of objectives.
   1.2. Define the deliverables and their requirements.
   1.3. Develop the project (manager's) charter.

Methodology Step 2. Define the Work

   2.1. Develop the WBS.
   2.2. Prepare the SOW.
   2.3. Prepare a product specification.

Methodology Step 3. Schedule Work, Resources, and Costs

   3.1. Define activities and activity duration.
   3.2. Develop a logic network and schedule.
   3.3. Assign and schedule resources and costs.
   3.4. Develop the cost estimate.
   3.5. Establish checkpoints and performance measures.
   3.6. Establish project baselines.
   3.7. Develop a project plan.
   3.8. Obtain approval of the project plan.

NEW CONTRACT

Replan

The implementation phase is identical to the generic model.

In some organizations, a dedicated proposal team prepares most proposals; therefore, a different cast of players is needed to implement the project. The new project participants will need to learn the project and most likely will recommend and require changes to the implementation and resource plans.

SCENARIO 6. STARTING A LIFE-CYCLE PROGRAM

This scenario assumes that the project/program manager starts with a blank page to proceed and develop a great idea for a new product. The program manager is given the go-ahead to evaluate the feasibility and to eventually manage the entire program if it is approved.

Scenario 6, Step 0. Project Phase in the Life Cycle

Starting a totally new project means starting with the initiation phase (also called the feasibility or conceptual phase). The phase usually begins with an idea or suggestion or is driven by the organization's need to meet some major objective. During this phase, alternatives are evaluated and selected using a standard problem-solving methodology or quantitative analysis. Depending on the organization, the business case must be made and presented, often involving economic, financial, and marketing analyses. At the end of this phase a deliverable is due that includes the results of any analyses, the beginnings of a project plan, a presentation to some level of decision-makers, and also should include a plan for the work to be performed in the next phase—the planning phase.

Figure 3.12 illustrates the program and its phases and subphases. The initiation or feasibility phase is planned as a project with its own initiation (In), planning (P), and implementation (Im) subphases, with the output or end item being a feasibility report that includes program planning items such as a WBS and preliminary schedule and plan for the next phase, the "planning phase."

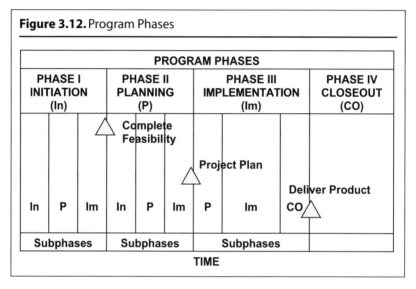

Figure 3.12. Program Phases

PROGRAM PHASES			
PHASE I **INITIATION** **(In)**	**PHASE II** **PLANNING** **(P)**	**PHASE III** **IMPLEMENTATION** **(Im)**	**PHASE IV** **CLOSEOUT** **(CO)**

Complete Feasibility

Project Plan

Deliver Product

In	P	Im	In	P	Im	P	Im	CO

Subphases	Subphases	Subphases	

TIME

The planning phase also could be managed as a project with (1) an initiation phase that represents an updating of feasibility analysis material, (2) planning the work in the phase, and (3) implementing the project to produce a project plan for the implementation phase. Phase III, Implementation, is the primary phase where the work is performed, but it would also include a subphase (P) of updating the project plan, (Im) implementing the plan, and preparing a closeout (CO) plan.

What is potentially confusing when discussing the generic project management methodology is that many of the items generated in the feasibility phase also are required in the planning phase and used in the implementation phase. For example, the objectives, requirements, initial WBS, and initial cost and schedule data for the implementation are initially generated in the initiation or feasibility phase and refined in the planning phase. Life-cycle cost data also may also be developed as part of the feasibility analysis and business case. The program WBS, like the program cost and schedule data, includes the feasibility, planning, and implementation phases as well as any subsequent phases that are part of the program.

A new project manager must determine the exact deliverable item or items that are required at the end of the initiation or feasibility phase and at the end of the planning phase—when they are expected—and the budget to develop them. A typical deliverable often includes a formal presentation to senior management as well as the results of the various analyses.

Through the planning subphase of the initiation phase, the work must be planned from two perspectives: (1) the immediate planning of the project to develop the deliverables at the end of the initiation phase, and (2) the program, consisting of the subsequent phases of implementation, closeout, and perhaps operation and maintenance. So there are two levels of planning: one for the short-term outputs to enable the program to proceed into the next phase and the broader planning for the total program.

Scenario 6, Step 1. Establish Project Objectives

The methodology for Scenario 6 focuses on the initiation phase work within a program framework.

1.1. Develop the statement of objectives.
1.2. Define the deliverables and their requirements.
1.3. Develop the project (manager's) charter.

Scenario 6, Step 1.1. Develop the Statement of Objectives, and Step 1.2.
Define the Deliverables and Their Requirements
The objective of the initiation phase is usually to perform
the necessary analyses to be able to make a recommendation
either to proceed or cancel the proposed program.

For Step 1.2, some organizations have clear procedures on
what analyses or output products are necessary to determine
feasibility. Often there is a requirement that the business
case demonstrate a certain minimum cost/benefit ratio or
minimum internal rate of return for projects to be funded
for planning and implementation. In other situations, the
deliverables may be an initial, preliminary plan or set of options and alternatives. The project manager must get agreement on what the deliverables are.

Scenario 6, Step 1.3. Develop the Project (Manager's) Charter
A minimum project manager's charter, focusing on the resources and goals of the initiation phase, is essential. This
becomes the precedent for the charters for the planning and
implementation phases.

Scenario 6, Step 2. Define the Work

> 2.1. Develop the WBS.
> 2.2. Develop the SOW.
> 2.3. Prepare the specification.

The work to be defined is what is necessary to prepare the
required documentation and presentation material to get
approval to proceed into the planning phase.

The WBS prepared should be a program WBS that defines
the scope of the total program, covering all life-cycle phases,
including the initiation phase effort. The initiation phase
WBS elements assist the project manager in defining the

scope of the work to be performed in this first phase and the framework for the schedule of the work to be performed in this phase. For small programs and projects, the WBS may be very simple, but it is still important.

Formal statements of work need to be prepared only for any elements of the work to be subcontracted or authorized to be performed by other organizations. In-house analyses usually are straightforward and use standard analysis methodologies, especially for smaller programs. The work schedule can be reviewed by the participants if there is concern regarding understanding of the work to be performed and the person or organization responsible. The project manager may use checklists to assign and track work.

The specifications of this phase's deliverables often take the form of organization or management requirements to get program approval at the end of the initiation phase. In more mature organizations, the type of work to be performed in the initiation phase is often specified in organizational procedures, and the performance targets are required analyses and presentation formats and instructions.

Preliminary specifications or performance requirements for the primary product to be delivered at the end of the implementation are usually an output of the initiation phase.

Scenario 6, Step 3. Schedule the Work and the Resources

3.1. Define activities and activity duration.
3.2. Develop a logic network and schedule.
3.3. Assign and schedule resources and costs.
3.4. Develop the cost estimate.
3.5. Establish checkpoints and performance measures.
3.6. Establish project baselines.
3.7. Develop a project plan.
3.8. Approve the project plan.

In Scenario 6 the focus is on the overall program and the initiation phase. Steps 3.1–3.5 are normal internal processes to schedule the work to be performed in this phase. MS Project® and other scheduling tools can be used if needed. Checklists and memos work well for very simple projects. Remember, this is only for the work to be performed in the feasibility phase, not the work in the subsequent phases.

Step 3.6 is performed when the project team and the project sponsor review and concur on the schedule and budget for the feasibility phase work.

Step 3.7 is really three steps and three plans. The first simply addresses the work in the initiation phase and may be very brief; the second addresses the work to be performed in the planning phase and may simply be a "next steps" section of the final product of the initiation phase. Both of these are prepared within the framework of the overall program plan, which is updated and expanded as the program gets increasingly defined and emphasizes the primary program output from the implementation phase. Obtaining approval of the overall concept and approval to proceed into the planning phase is the goal of the feasibility phase. An initial and preliminary program plan may be one of the deliverables.

The "Rules for a Successful Proposal" presented in Scenario 4 also apply here (see Figure 3.5). The project manager for a new project is usually its primary advocate, and following these rules is important to getting approval of the overall concept and for moving on to the next phase.

Step 3.8 is the important review and acceptance of the program plan and other justification documents.

The same tactics are followed for the planning phase of the program: It is treated like a project in its own right. The end item is a project plan for the implementation phase and approval to proceed.

SCENARIO 7: TAKE OVER AN ONGOING PROJECT

The current project manager was reassigned, and a new project manager takes over the work in the middle of the project.

Scenario 7, Step 0. Project Phase in the Life Cycle

Where does the new project manager start? When a new project manager is assigned, it is essential for that person to know which life-cycle phase the project is in and which of the preceding six scenarios best describes the project setting. Whichever scenario is applicable, it is critical to know two major items:

1. The required *output:* what the project deliverables are; what commitments have been made; and what the expected performance of the deliverables is

2. The available *input:* what budget and resources are available, what commitments have been made, and what has been authorized.

The takeover project manager faces four categories of problems:

1. *Environmental*—Before the new project manager assumes responsibility for the project, make sure the person assigning the new project manager addresses all the environmental considerations (see Part 4) and that they are included in the project charter as necessary. This includes management support, software and technology, and supporting procedures and directives or equivalent.

2. *Core Process*—Verify that your predecessor has followed the steps in the methodology presented in this book. It is important to make sure the project manager's charter

addresses the resources and authority to perform the job. Ensure that the necessary project management products are developed, and finish them as necessary. This includes the WBS, SOW, schedule, and budget. Determine the cost and schedule status of the deliverables, then continue the remaining steps of the methodology to complete the project. It is important to replan and refinance as soon as possible so that the project becomes viable if these elements part of the problem. (See Figure 3.11 in Scenario 5 for the replanning approach.) As the project manager, you do not want to take on responsibility for a sinking ship without a recovery plan. The best strategy may be a total review and replanning of the project.

3. *Facilitating*—Part 4 of this book presents discussions of five facilitating elements: human resource management, risk management, communications management, project procurement management, and configuration management. The status of the application of these elements should be reviewed to ensure that they are being applied effectively.

4. *Personnel*—Many personnel issues are beyond the scope of those addressed in the Human Resource Management section in Part 4. Use the bibliography for additional advice and recommendations on identifying and resolving personnel problems.

A project manager taking over a railroad construction project sent a memorandum of understanding to his department head that addressed most of the items recommended in the project manager's charter. After discussion with him and reaching concurrence, the memorandum served very well when support was needed from other managers.

REFERENCES

1. Gregory T. Haugan. *Project Planning and Scheduling* (Vienna, VA: Management Concepts, Inc., 2002), p. 78.
2. U.S. Department of Defense. *Handbook for Preparation of Statement of Work* (MIL-HDBK-245D, 3 April 1996), pp. 25–28.
3. Ibid., p. 27.
4. Peter S. Cole. *How to Write a Statement of Work.* 5th ed. (Vienna, VA: Management Concepts, Inc., 2003) .
5. See Part 4, Section 5 discussion of U.S. Department of Defense, *Handbook for Preparation of Statement of Work* (MIL-HDBK-245D, 3 April 1996).
6. Invitations for bids (IFBs) and requests for quotations (RFQs) are other procurement processes. These focus on price and are used for well defined "off-the-shelf" products requiring no development. See Marshall R. Engelbeck, *Acquisition Management* (Vienna, VA: Management Concepts, Inc., 2002), p. 141.
7. See Michael G. Martin, *Delivering Project Excellence with the Statement of Work* (Vienna, VA: Management Concepts, Inc., 2003), p. 35, for a further discussion of proposal statements of work.

PART 4

Environmental and Facilitating Elements

Project management basics are multidimensional and include consideration of the environment in which the project manager must operate. In addition, five "facilitating elements" should be considered for implementation concurrently with implementation of the basic project management process, where applicable. These elements add other dimensions to the basic methodology and cut across all the steps. They are:

Human Resource Management: The processes of resource acquisition and planning, roles and responsibilities of participants, and organization structures

Risk Management: The process of identifying, addressing, and managing risks in a disciplined framework

Communications Management: Important aspects of the mechanisms of communication among stakeholders

Project Procurement Management: The typical and generic steps in the process of outsourcing work

Configuration Management: The process and discipline of managing project change.

The application of recognized and standard principles of project management in each of the facilitating elements significantly improves the chances for success and the quality and performance of project management—and thus the likelihood of success.

ENVIRONMENTAL ELEMENTS

- *Management Support*—to aid the project and project manager
- *Project Management Software*—tools to assist the project manager
- *Procedures and Directives*—include authority for the project manager and descriptions of how the project should be managed within the larger enterprise; also include the project management methodology

We all want to work in a friendly, professional, supportive environment where the overall organization is mature in its use and application of good project management principles and practices. In a mature organization, management support is more or less automatic, and the managers understand the role they must play to support their project managers. (Several methods are generally used to determine the level of project management maturity in an organization and thereby identify areas for improvement. As stated earlier, this book is based on enabling the reader to bring the organization to a "Level 2" stage of maturity.[1,2])

The environmental elements should be in place before the start of the project. However, they can be put in place any time and may be covered in the project charter, as addressed in Part 2. The most important of them is the first one—your supervisor or project sponsor must provide support and assistance to you (or keep out of your way).

Management Support

Management support[3] must be available on a continual basis so that the project manager can receive the needed resources, policy guidance, and assistance. This is required initially and on an ongoing basis during the project execution and is especially important in an organizational environment where support from other functional managers is required.

Management support refers primarily to the effort the project sponsor or supervisor makes in assisting and mentoring the project manager and also includes upper management's willingness to continually improve the project management process. The project sponsor is often the project manager's supervisor but may be anyone of power in the organization.

The project sponsor is one of several persons who have responsibilities to the project manager. This person is aware of his or her responsibilities and what support the project manager expects.

Figure 4.1 lists the most important of these responsibilities.

Figure 4.1. Project Sponsor Responsibilities

1. *Ensure the project is funded and resources assigned at the appropriate level upon initiation*—Project funding is not usually a problem when you have been awarded a contract; however, getting the resources assigned is always a problem.
2. *Understand the principles and methodology of project management*—Be aware of the methodology using to manage the project and be familiar with the terminology.
3. *Conduct oversight functions through reviews and reports*—While the project manager may not want anyone looking over his or her shoulder and few persons like to prepare progress reports, these are important activities to keep the sponsor involved so that the sponsor is available and knowledgeable to assist in solving problems when they arise.
4. *Serve as the senior level liaison for the project*—Many projects require resources from other organizations or are performed for other organizations. The project sponsor is normally in a position to communicate and negotiate with other senior managers to resolve resource conflicts and establish priorities.
5. *Conduct project reviews*—On smaller projects the sponsor may ask the project manager to provide a briefing on status and problems; as the projects get larger, these briefings may be more formal and include senior managers from throughout the organization. These reviews are normally useful for the project manager so that problems can be addressed and policy items resolved at the appropriate level.

continues

Figure 4.1. Project Sponsor Responsibilities (continued)

---

6. *Guide the project manager, as appropriate, in project matters*—When the project manager is relatively inexperienced, having a mentoring relationship with the sponsor is beneficial. Note that this item is to "guide" and not to "micromanage."
7. *Provide additional funding and resources when justified*—Changes occur, and problems are not always foreseen; additional funding or resources, therefore, are sometimes required and may be needed to take advantage of opportunities. There must be a process or awareness on the part of the sponsor so that changes can be addressed and additional funding or resources made available when justified.
8. *Recommend cancellation of ineffective projects*—One of the responsibilities of the sponsor is to terminate the project when it appears the objectives cannot be met in a timely and cost-effective manner. The project manager often is too close to the problem to be objective, and it is necessary for projects to be canceled from time to time.

One communications firm in Northern Virginia has established a Vice President for Project Management to facilitate the support needed by the various project managers from the functional managers.

The items in Figure 4.1 are also a requirement for the customer project manager when the project is being performed for another organization. (See Part 3, Scenarios 1, 2, and 5.) But what do you do if the sponsor or higher management is unaware of their responsibilities or of what assistance you need, or is just too busy (or inept)? Or your organization's level of maturity is at Level 1 or worse? Solving these problems is one of the purposes of the project manager's charter prepared in Step 1.3 of the methodology and described in Part 2.

In a project management training program provided to a group of IT personnel in Arizona, attendees indicated that it would be very useful if the senior management were apprised of their responsibilities. When approached, the company president concurred, and a special executive-level course on project management was provided to the president and all of the other senior managers.

Project Management Software

It is important to select or use available project management software to provide discipline, facilitate planning, process data, and prepare control and status reports. All project management software is designed to be compatible with the methodology described in this book. The software and computer system must be suitable for the project. In general, most projects you would be managing do not require software costing several thousands of dollars. Personnel experienced or trained in project management software should be available; many courses are also available to assist new users.

All projects in an organization should use the same standard software so that experience in using a specific application package can be developed and transferred and common data can be readily interchanged. Similarly, when work is outsourced it is important to require that the organization performing the work uses project management software that is compatible with the software the client or customer uses to facilitate communications and reporting.

In these days of the Internet and local and wide area networks, most users want to be able to use a common software package with the project data available to the project team and the ability for team members to provide status data directly into the program. Networked project management software is especially useful when project resources are dispersed geographically and when telecommuting is practiced. Each project manager and team member should be proficient in using the software.

Issue Procedures and Directives

As they grow in project management maturity, most organizations recognize that they need internal procedures and directives to address organizational issues and responsibilities. Often these are appended to the organization manual and are part of the position descriptions of the various managers described in the manual. Organizations experienced in managing projects issue procedures and directives so that the stakeholders of a project understand the organization's policy regarding how projects should be organized and managed and what the responsibilities are of the project manager, team members, sponsor, other managers, and the supporting organizations.

Procedures and directives can be informal, such as memoranda from the appropriate level of the organization, or a formal document. The procedures should reference or document the methodology and the responsibilities for performing or supporting each step. They follow each step of the methodology and describe how it is to be accomplished, including the forms, approvals, and timing.

> In a large U.S. government agency, the project management methodology of one of the large projects is being used as a prototype for future projects. The project manager was asked to document the procedures that were used successfully in a format that could be readily converted into formal procedures and directives.

HUMAN RESOURCE MANAGEMENT

> Definition: The processes of resource acquisition and planning; defining roles and responsibilities of participants, including the customer, project team, and upper management; and defining organization structures.

Much human resource management is mechanical—processes oriented to make sure the human resources are available to support the project manager, are organized, and understand their roles. The other side—motivation, leadership, conflicts, and relationships—is not addressed in-depth in this book, but is yet another dimension.[4]

Peter Drucker discusses this very important facet of human resource management extensively. His work and the work of F.W. Taylor and Henry Gantt[5] put it in the context of the project manager.

One can learn certain skills in managing people—for example, the skill to lead a conference, conduct an interview, or follow a methodology. One can set down practices that are conducive to improvement—in the structure of the relationship among the project manager and members of the project team and supporting organizations, in a promotion system, or in the rewards and incentives of an organization. But developing and improving persons as individuals still requires a basic quality that the project manager cannot create by supplying skills or emphasizing the importance of the task. It requires integrity of character.

There is emphasis within organizations on liking people, helping people, and getting along with people as qualifications for a project manager. These alone are never enough. Peter Drucker states: "In every successful organization there is one boss who does not like people, who does not help them, and who does not get along with them. Cold, unpleasant, demanding, he often teaches and develops more men than anyone else. He commands more respect than the most likable man ever could. He demands exacting workmanship of himself as well as of his men. He sets high standards and expects that they will be lived up to. He considers only what is right and never who is right. And though often himself a man of brilliance, he never rates intellectual brilliance above integrity in others. The manager who lacks these qualities of character—no matter how likable, helpful, or amiable, no matter even how competent or brilliant—is a menace and should be adjudged 'unfit to be a manager and a gentleman.'"[6]

What a project manager does can be analyzed systematically and is presented as the project management methodology. As mentioned, this book focuses on the mechanical processes that can be learned, but not on the human relation skills nor on the one qualification that the project manager cannot acquire but must bring to the work place: character.

Human Resource Management Process

Human resource management activities are directed internally within the project to make sure that the team members are available, ready, willing, and able to perform their expected activities. The focus is to ensure the input to the project is adequate to provide the output and meet objectives.

In general management terms, this is referred to as the function of staffing which comprises those activities that are essential in manning and in keeping manned, the positions provided for by the organization structure.[7] It thus encompasses the activities of defining the personnel requirements necessary for the job to be done; the activities of inventorying, appraising, and selecting candidates for positions; and the activities of training or otherwise developing both candidates and incumbents to accomplish their tasks as effectively as possible.

Figure 4.2 illustrates the human resource management process. The steps in this process are ongoing throughout the life of the project:

A.1 *Define Resource Requirements*—includes determination of the specific skills required for each activity, the overall quantity of each skill, how people are to be organized, and the schedule of when people are needed

A.2 *Acquire Resources*—involves hiring or coordinating personnel assignments with functional managers and replacing personnel because of normal turnover; this is a continuous activity

A.3 *Train the Resources*—involves individual training of project personnel to address both an understanding of each team member's roles within the project and improvement in his or her functional and professional skills

A.4 *Develop the Team*—involves group activities to increase team performance and maintain team morale.

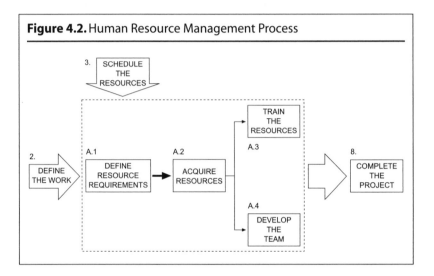

Figure 4.2. Human Resource Management Process

Organization Structures

The management function of organization for the project manager involves: (1) the determination and enumeration of the activities required to achieve the objectives of the project, (2) the grouping of these activities, (3) the assignment of such groups of activities to an organizational entity headed by a manager, and (4) the delegation of authority to carry them out.

The organization structure is, of course, not an end in itself but a tool for accomplishing project objectives. Efficient organization will contribute to the project's success. The organization must fit the task and must reflect the compromises and limitations imposed on the project manager.

Three key factors in the probability of a successful project are: (1) the culture and environment (as discussed in Part 2), (2) the project manager's ability to follow the methodology presented in this book, and (3) the quality of the people performing the work. Project managers rarely are able to set up the type of organization they prefer. They have limited influence on the environment, have some influence over the persons working on the project, and must be able to implement the methodology. The actual organization structure is not important to the success of the project, but these three items are critical. Nonetheless, it is important to understand something about the various organization structures to assist in managing projects within each general type.

The three major types of relevant organization structures are functional, project, and matrix.

Functional

The functional organization is the traditional structure in which the members of the organization are grouped by specialty and managed as functional units. Examples of the functions are marketing, manufacturing, quality assurance, engineering, and finance. Within each organization are more functional units, such as mechanical engineers, civil engineers, and aeronautical engineers. Functional organizations have projects, but the scope of the projects is limited to the boundaries of the function.

For example, the engineering department in a functional organization will do its work and manage its projects independent of the manufacturing or marketing departments. It will cooperate with other organizations and request input but not rely on the resources of any other organizations to perform any of the project work. The output of the functional departments is provided as input to other functional departments; for example, the engineering department provides drawings to the manufacturing department.

This organization structure is likely to be used in Scenario 1 projects—Direct Assignment from Supervisor.

Project

The pure project organization is an independent entity separate from other organizational entities in the enterprise. If the overall enterprise is organized in a project format, the managers and workers are all grouped into independent "vertical" projects. Because each project is independent, some of the conflicts and other problems generally experienced in the functional organization structure are avoided. The project manager has total authority over the project and retains the flexibility to acquire resources needed for the project either within or outside of the parent organization subject only to time, cost, and performance constraints identified as project goals and objectives. Personnel are assigned to the project and report directly to the project manager.

Project managers like this organization because it gives them complete control over the resources they need for the project. There is a clear unity of command, and because the project personnel usually are located together, communications are efficient.

The structure within the project organization has personnel grouped by functions, with the specific functions related to the needs of the project, such as engineers, editors and writers, lawyers, programmers, buyers, or laborers, depending on the project. However, this structure is relatively inefficient if there are several independent projects within an organization because of the duplication of functions, the difficulty in hiring or locating certain specialist persons for short periods of time, and problems in reassigning or laying people off when their work is completed and during the closeout phase. This structure is common in large, multiyear construction projects in which subcontractors perform many of the functions, the work is largely outsourced, and only the management team remains with the project from the beginning to the end.

This organization structure is likely to occur in Scenario 3—Outsourcing, and Scenario 5—Perform to a Contract. In the latter case, the parent organization may have been successful in a large construction contract for which it was the construction manager.

Matrix

The matrix organization structure is the most common. It is a relatively new organizational construct, while the functional and pure project organizations go back centuries. In the matrix organization, the project manager is required to use resources from other organizations, usually functional organizations, to perform the work on the project. The matrix concept has many variations.

The key aspect of the matrix concept is the authority relationships and the relationships of the supporting resources. The following types of matrix organizations progress from the "weakest" to the "strongest" in terms of project manager authority. None of the configurations relates directly to whether or not a project will be successful, with "success" defined as meeting the project objectives and satisfying the customer or sponsor.

Expeditor—The authority exists in a top-level manager who is not directly involved in the day-to-day operations of the project and with the working persons assigned to the project. The project manager is simply an expeditor who reminds the assigned personnel when activities are to be completed and expects that they will comply. The "expeditor" is usually a lower-level staff person. Project management methodology usually is not involved—only internal, informal working relationships.

This organization structure would be likely for Scenario 1— Direct Assignment from Supervisor.

Coordinator—The sponsor or a senior manager, perhaps the CEO, assigns a person to "coordinate" the work of several persons or organizations to achieve the project goals. The person works under the authority of the sponsor and may be partially following the project management methodology.

This organization structure would be likely for Scenario 1— Direct Assignment from Supervisor.

Normal Matrix—A project manager is assigned the responsibility for the project and is expected to follow the project management methodology using the resources of the functional organizations. Steps 1–3 are performed collegially in accordance with the culture of the organization and upper management support.

This organization structure would be likely for any of the scenarios.

Strong Matrix—A project manager is assigned the responsibility for the project and is expected to follow the project management methodology. However, the project manager has full budget authority and may or may not use the resources of the functional organizations, depending upon their capability and likely degree of cooperation.

This organization structure would be likely for any scenario.

In addition to the three items mentioned as requirements for a successful project, three elements assist the project manager when working in a matrix environment:

1. The project manager's charter becomes critical and needs to emphasize and guarantee the support and resources provided by the functional organizations.

2. The project management methodology and process needs to involve the functional organizations in all phases of the project, especially in Step 3, where the work and resources are scheduled.

3. There must be an internal process or culture that holds all persons and organizations assigned accountable for the success of each project.

The third item implies that performance evaluations of functional managers include considering the contribution they make to the success of the projects they support. This is important because functional managers often are evaluated on meeting objectives related only to their areas of specialty. As such, it is only natural for them to be reluctant to lend resources to another organization and thereby reduce their own effectiveness and performance level.

Virtual Teams

With the rapid increase in the use of the Internet to communicate within and between organizations and with increased telecommuting, the number of virtual project teams also has grown rapidly. A virtual project team can be described and defined several ways, but basically it involves an organizational construct wherein some or all of the members of the project team are not only not colocated, but may be thousands of miles apart.

While the methodology presented in this book must still be followed, additional procedures and discipline are required to accommodate the unique requirements of virtual teams. These include accounting for language differences, time zones, culture, and internal operating procedures among and within the elements of the virtual team. Any of the scenarios can be managed using virtual teams.[8]

Project Participants' Roles and Responsibilities

There are several categories of participants in a project, with different roles and responsiblities.

Project Stakeholders

Project stakeholders are individuals and organizations who are actively involved in the project or whose interests may be affected by it. The project management team must identify the stakeholders, determine their needs and expectations, and manage and influence these expectations to ensure a successful project. The many different names and categories of project stakeholders include: customers and sponsors, internal and external, owners and funders, suppliers and contractors, team members, government agencies, media, individual citizens, and society at large.

Managing stakeholder expectations may be difficult because stakeholders often have different objectives.

Project Sponsor

The project sponsor is the person to whom the project manager reports for direction and for allocation of funds. The project sponsor is typically a senior executive in the organization.

Some of the project sponsor's major roles and responsibilities are to:

• Ensure that the project is funded at the appropriate level upon initiation

• Conduct oversight through reviews and reports

• Serve as the senior-level liaison for the project

- Conduct/attend project reviews

- Guide the project manager, as appropriate, in project matters

- Provide additional funding, when justified

- Recommend cancellation of ineffective projects.

Customer

Projects always are accomplished for customers, be they internal or external to the organization. The customer may be the sponsor, or it may be several persons or organizations. The project manager must proactively involve the customers because:

- It may not be clear who your "customer" is.

- The customers may not state their requirements clearly or completely.

- You do not know their jobs; therefore, you cannot know their problems.

- Their concept of the solution may not solve the problem.

- They may have unspoken expectations by which your efforts will be judged.

- If the customers are not part of the planning process, they may be reluctant to accept the solution.

- All of your customers may not talk to each other; so you must talk to all of them.

- You may begin to give them what you think they want instead of what they say they need.

- What they say they need may not be what they actually need.

In the relationship between the project manager and the customer, the project manager must be a good communicator and use leadership ability to represent the organization and the project in the best way possible. The customer can help solve many of the project manager's problems but must be kept properly informed and up-to-date. Also, remember that the definition of "quality" is "what the customer expects."

Project Manager

The project manager must make things happen. The behavior of the project manager can make or break many projects. Senior management looks to the project manager for "success," however defined. Peers and subordinates look for orders, guidance, correction, support, and praise. Some of the project manager's major roles and responsibilities are to:

- Implement a logical and consistent project management methodology

- Define the project and obtain approvals

- Ensure customer satisfaction

- Perform day-to-day activities

- Take initiatives

- Negotiate commitments regarding:

    —Quality

    —Cost

    —Schedule

    —Product performance

- Ensure achievement of forecast benefits

- Communicate the methodology and expectations.

Project Team Members
Each project team member also has responsibilities. As Dr. W. Edwards Deming stated, "improved quality is achieved by the actions of everyone in concert."[9] Each team member, in a sense, is actually a project manager, but on a smaller scale, applying project management principles to his or her specific activities. Team members also must accept responsibility for their assignments and perform them to the best of their abilities.

Major duties of project team members are to:

- Participate in planning and replanning

- Be committed to the project

- Manage assigned activities

- Coordinate activities with the project manager

- Provide status reports

- Alert the project manager to potential problems

- Meet commitments.

Program Manager
In this book we have been consistent in our use of "program manager" versus "project manager":

Program Manager—responsible for all life-cycle phases and also may also be responsible for a "family" of projects

Project Manager—responsible for work on a project, defined as "a temporary endeavor undertaken to create a unique product, service, or result."

A program manager, therefore, would be a person who manages the program through all its life cycle phases and manages each phase him- or herself or uses project managers for each phase, as shown in Figure 4.3.

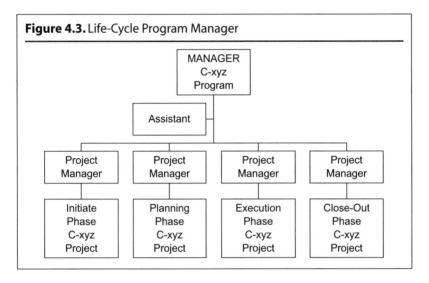

Figure 4.3. Life-Cycle Program Manager

Note that the program is large enough to plan each phase as if it were an independent project. The actual person identified as the project manager could be the same person for each phase.

The second definition of a program manager is a person who manages several projects that are all oriented toward the same program goal and may have several project managers reporting to him or her. Each project may be in a different life-cycle phase; the "program" frequently is long term. An example is a program to reduce highway fatalities that may include a large number of individual projects. This organization is shown in Figure 4.4.

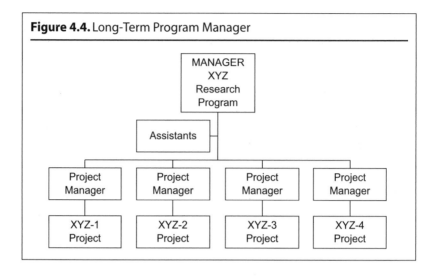

Figure 4.4. Long-Term Program Manager

RISK MANAGEMENT

Risk management activities are designed to assist the project manager and team members in understanding project risks and the probability and consequences of failure, and to plan appropriate responses. Risks can be either internal or external to the project, and risk analysis addresses both good and bad (opportunities and risks).

Risk management is an ongoing iterative process that follows the life cycle. Risk planning is performed at a high level during the initial phases and at increasing levels of detail as the planning phase is implemented. Budgets and schedules are created considering risk mitigation, and project risk management techniques are used in the implementation phases of project. The results and effectiveness of the risk management activities are included in the final documentation of lessons learned.

Risk management activities include determining what is necessary to mitigate and control the risks. Risk planning consists of the up-front activities necessary to execute a successful risk management program. It is an integral part of normal program planning and management and is an ongoing activity that is performed throughout the project life cycle.

The nature of the implementation of a risk management program within a project depends on the size of the project and the level of the organization's maturity. Sophisticated schedule and cost risk software using Monte Carlo simulation and other tools is available. These tools operate as add-ons to the normal project management software. Like all tools, they follow and support the process.

Definitions

Risk is a measure of the inability to achieve overall program objectives within defined cost, schedule, and technical constraints. Risk has two components: (1) the probability of failing to achieve a particular outcome and (2) the consequences or impacts of failing to achieve that outcome. Or stated a simpler way: (1) the probability that the risk item will happen, and (2) the resulting impact on the overall project objectives.

Risk items are those events within the project that, if they go wrong, could result in problems in meeting the project's objectives. Risk items are defined to the degree that the risk and causes are understandable and can be assessed in terms of probability/likelihood and consequence/impact to establish the level of risk.

Technical risk is the risk associated with the evolution of the project work affecting the level of performance necessary to meet the specified requirements of the deliverable items or the operational requirements. In projects without explicit specifications, technical risk and quality risk are synonymous and refer to the risk associated with the ability to meet the customer's or sponsor's expectations or other quality criteria.

Cost risk normally is associated with the program's ability to achieve its life-cycle cost objectives. Two risk areas bearing on this definition of cost are: (1) the risk that the cost estimates and objectives are accurate and reasonable and (2) the risk that program execution will not meet the cost objectives as a result of a failure to handle cost, schedule, and performance risks.

Schedule risks are those associated with the adequacy of the time estimated and allocated for the project duration and delivery of required end items. Two risk areas bearing on schedule risk are: (1) the risk that the schedule estimates and objectives are realistic and not reasonable and (2) the risk that program execution will fall short of the schedule objectives as a result of failure to handle cost, schedule, or performance risks.

Risk Management Process

The generic process for risk analysis is illustrated in Figure 4.5. For simplicity, this book focuses on the four core steps in a risk management program. (Obviously, the first step is to plan your work and plan the risk program.) The PMBOK® Guide includes a discussion of six processes, leading off with risk management planning and separating qualitative risk analysis from quantitative risk analysis.[10] Other authors identify five processes.[11]

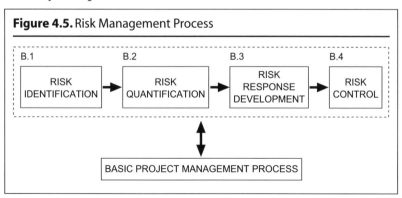

Figure 4.5. Risk Management Process

B.1 *Risk Identification*—consists of determining sources of risk and risk events that may be expected to affect the project.

B.2 *Risk Quantification*—involves determining which risk events warrant response.

The combination of these first two steps is a classic SWOT analysis (Strengths, Weaknesses, Opportunities, and Threats) that includes evaluation of internal and external factors in a performance audit. The internal performance audit examines the project's current performance in terms of meeting cost, schedule, and performance objectives and projecting and forecasting likely future performance. It also involves identifying specific sources of potential degradation of the ability to meet project objectives.

Risk analysis and performance audits also include consideration of forces and conditions outside the project that may affect success in reaching project goals.

B.3 *Risk Response Development*—is the process of determining the specific actions to be taken as a result of the first two steps. This includes avoidance—eliminating a particular threat; mitigation—reducing the impact of the threat; or retention—accepting the consequences if they occur. Risk response development also may be positive, where opportunities, in addition to threats, are pursued.

B.4 *Risk Control*—is the process of initiating corrective action, such as implementing a contingency plan and constantly updating the risk management plan, as the project is implemented and anticipated risk events occur or fail to occur.

One feature of the project management methodology is the definition of CCPs during Step 3.5, Establish Checkpoints and Performance Measures. At each one of these CCPs, a risk analysis should be performed. In addition, risk analyses of varying comprehensiveness are performed as part of the activity at each of the other major steps.

Risk analyses are either quantitative or qualitative. Quantitative analysis is based on the use of the logic network, modeling, and probability analysis, and qualitative analysis is based on the knowledge, experience, and intuition of the project team members and stakeholders. The quantitative approach appears to be most useful on the larger projects where the value of the output is consistent with the analysis effort required. Software is available to incorporate both types of analyses into a risk management program.

The types of risk fall into two categories: scope risk and resource risk. Scope risk is the risk that the team will not be able to physically produce the project's deliverables that meet the performance requirements. Resource risk is the risk that the team won't be able to produce the deliverables on time, or within the staffing or spending limits specified by the sponsor. Projects with scope risk problems usually have resource risk problems as well.

The key to any risk management program is the ability to identify and evaluate risks. The two most difficult aspects to risk management are: (1) identifying the risks and (2) establishing priorities. This assumes, of course, that the project manager has the discipline to implement a risk management process.

Risk Identification
Risk identification deserves special attention. Common sense is involved, and the experience of the project team and other stakeholders is important in the identification process. The difficulty is that there are too many choices. All of the activities on the schedule occur in the future, so there is some risk regarding schedule completion of every activity.

No matter how the cost estimate was determined or the resource requirements estimated, there is some risk regarding the accuracy of the estimate—at every level.

If a WBS was not used to define the scope, some important work may not have been priced. Each WBS element, work package, and activity has some risk. Many assumptions are always made in planning the project—for example, availability of funding or availability of key personnel or facilities—that add some element of risk.

Over 25 years ago an article in Fortune magazine featured a discussion with a senior manager from Lockheed regarding cost overruns on aerospace projects and why they occurred. The response was essentially, "it is not the unknowns that are the problem, but the unknown unknowns."[12] This is a difficulty with risk analysis—that you identify all the major risks and the appropriate response and a totally unanticipated element arises. These are the "unknown unknowns"—the ones we don't know that we don't know, and your project is all of a sudden in trouble. It is important to recognize that this might occur; it also is important to have a risk management program so that those risks that are identified are effectively addressed.

Each project is unique and at the same time is similar to other projects, especially in the same organization. So this is where experience comes in to play.

The intent of the risk identification step in the risk management process is to come up with a list of all the sources of risk and risk events that may be expected to affect the project significantly. This can be accomplished in many ways. Some items may come from the "lessons learned" document prepared in Step 10.4 on other projects in the organization. The preferred approach is to use the project team and as many other experienced persons and stakeholders as possible in the process.

Each risk item has two factors associated with it: (1) the probability that the risk event will occur and a stated requirement is not met and (2) the severity of the impact of the risk event on the project objectives.

Risk identification is accomplished by an organized and comprehensive survey of all project areas that could engender risk to the project. To encompass the entire project, project key elements are reviewed.

In these meetings, the typical documents and plans to be reviewed include:

- SOWs and delivery requirements

- Contract requirements

- Performance specifications

- Work breakdown structure

- Test and evaluation plans

- Master schedules

- Management plans

- Production and facility plans

- Experience from similar projects

- Lessons learned documents.

Risk Assessment

Risk assessment is a process by which potential problems and identified risks are analyzed and quantified to classify the risks according to their potential severity. This step can get very complex and sophisticated; however, a simple exercise can be used to identify and establish priorities for risk items on small to medium projects:[13]

1. Assemble the project team and others. Assign a facilitator.

2. Use the WBS as a framework and brainstorm a list of possible risk elements. Do not be restricted to the WBS, but use it as a place to start discussion. Use other documents as well.

3. List the potential risk items on a flipchart. The order is not important at this step.

4. For each risk item on the list, assign a probability number of the likelihood of it happening.

5. For each risk item, assign a number from 1 to 5 to indicate the degree of the impact on the project should the risk occur. The higher number, the higher the impact.

6. For each risk item, multiply the risk probability by the risk impact factor to arrive at a risk index.

7. Rank the items by the risk index. The higher number would be the most risky.

8. Discuss and identify reasonable responses to reduce the threat posed by each risk.

This is a "poor man's" approach to risk identification, quantification, and response development—the first three steps in the risk management process of Figure 4.5.[14]

One of the most valuable outputs of this exercise is the focus of the project team, at least for a short time, on where the risks are. This is important input to the project manager and also starts the process of continuous risk evaluation.

You can use these steps for assessing risk for any type of project—simple or complex, small or large. Leading the team through the steps builds understanding of what the potential problems might be and agreement about how the team will prevent them from occurring.

Developing a Risk Response

After the program's risks have been identified, assessed, and ranked, the approach to handling each significant risk must be developed (Step 8 in the exercise). There are essentially four techniques or options for handling risks: avoidance, control, transfer, and assumption. For all identified risks, the various handling techniques should be evaluated in terms of feasibility, expected effectiveness, cost and schedule implications, and the effect on the objectives of the project.

For the items classified as high risk, as well as selected medium-risk items, a solution is prepared and documented. A comprehensive solution for a major potential problem could include the following: what must be done, the level of effort and materials required, the estimated cost to implement the plan, a proposed alternative schedule showing the proposed start date, the time phasing of significant risk reduction activities, the completion date, recommended metrics for tracking the action, a list of all assumptions, and the person responsible for implementing and tracking the selected option. Making sure that someone is responsible for the action and that the person is aware he or she is responsible is an important step.

Risk Control

Assigning individual responsibility for each risk item is crucial to effective risk monitoring. Project team members are the "front line" for obtaining indications that risk-handling efforts are achieving their desired effects. Each person is responsible for monitoring and reporting the effectiveness of the handling actions for the risks assigned.

Risk will be made an agenda item at each project review, providing an opportunity for all concerned to offer suggestions for the best approach to managing it. Communicating risk increases the program's credibility and allows early actions to minimize adverse consequences or impacts.

A "watch list" should be prepared that includes all the identified risks, risk level, responsible person, and current status. Figure 4.6 presents a sample format.

Figure 4.6. Sample Risk Item Watch List

No.	RISK ITEM	RISK REDUCTION ACTIONS	RESP	DUE DATE	DATE COMPLETE	NOTES
1.						
2.						
Etc.						

COMMUNICATIONS MANAGEMENT AND COORDINATION

Communications management is the process of ensuring timely and appropriate generation, collection, dissemination, storage, and ultimate disposition of project information. Communications are both internal within the project and external. They are necessary for synchronizing and coordinating work on the project.

Communications are constant. The purposes of this facilitating element of the project management methodology are to: (1) ensure that those aspects of communication necessary for coordinating and successfully attaining the project objectives are addressed in an orderly and comprehensive manner, and (2) point out that the project manager must be proactive in the use of communications and coordination and realize their importance as an area of focus.

Communications Management Process

Figure 4.7 illustrates the continuous communications management process.

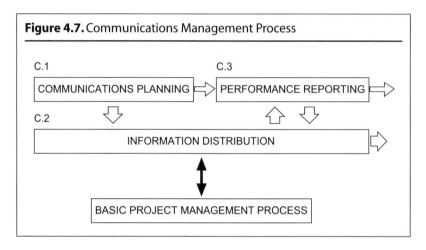

Figure 4.7. Communications Management Process

C.1 *Communications Planning*—occurs during the first three steps of the overall project management process, when the information and communication needs of the stakeholders, including the project manager and the project sponsor, are determined. Decisions are made regarding who needs what information, when they will need it, and how they will receive it.

C.2 *Information Distribution*—occurs throughout the project. The communication system must make sure that needed information is available in a timely manner to all stakeholders, including the project manager and the sponsor, so that necessary coordination can occur.

C.3 *Performance Reporting*—begins when the work starts on the project, usually when planning activities are completed. Performance reporting is a multimedia event, tailored to the audience. It includes reporting activity schedule status to the project manager and reporting project status at a critical checkpoint review or other project review. This is the feedback from the project team that is part of the coordination process.

The communications link between the project manager and the immediate project team is very important. Many of the problems with projects are lack of coordination, which arises out of simple and preventable communication problems. Some project managers hold regular, weekly "cadence" reviews to ensure tight coordination and status monitoring.

There are many references and other sources of study material available on the subject of communications within an organization and within a project. Communications often require "people skills." In this book, we tend to focus on technology, tools, the core methodologies, and the facilitating elements, but problems with these are not the only reasons projects fail. Flannes and Levin state: "They fail because of people. . . . Leadership and people skills . . . are also essential to project success."[15]

Need for Communication and Coordination[16]

The need to synchronize individual action on a project is obvious and is achieved by performing Steps 1, 2, and 3 with members of the project team. This process irons out differences in opinion as to how the project goals can be reached and any conflicts between individual motives and project objectives. Even where motives and objectives tend to be the same, individuals often see their own interests in somewhat different ways, and their actions to accomplish goals usually do not automatically mesh with the activities of others. It thus becomes the central task of the project manager to reconcile differences in approach, effort, or interest and to harmonize individual goals and actions so that they will bring about group objectives.

There is a tendency to ignore a fundamental truth that the best coordination occurs when individuals see how their jobs and their goals harmonize with the project's goals. This, in turn, implies knowledge and understanding of project objectives, not just on the part of a few at the top but by all stakeholders. If, for example, team members are not sure whether the basic goal of the project is cost containment, quality and performance of the deliverables, schedule discipline, a balance between them, or some other goal, it is virtually impossible to coordinate their efforts. Each would be guided by his or her own ideas of what is in the interest of the project or, without any such conviction, work for self-aggrandizement.

Principles of Coordination

One of the classic scholars on the concept of coordination, Mary Parker Follett,[17] differentiated principles from techniques and clarified the conditions for effective coordination.

The first principle is that coordination must be achieved through interpersonal, horizontal relationships of people in an enterprise. People exchange ideas, ideals, prejudices, and purposes through direct personal communication much more efficiently than by any other method. With the understanding gained in this way, they find means to achieve both project and personal goals. This recognized identity of ultimate interests then tends to bring agreement on methods and actions of achieving project goals.

For example, rivalry and consequent criticism, which all too frequently mar the relationships among members of the project team who come from different functional organizations, are the result and evidence of poor coordination and a lack of trust. The different functional personnel supporting the project bring different perspectives and backgrounds to the project. Unless the personnel of these organizations exchange ideas and reach an understanding, there can be no coordination among them. The project manager must act as a facilitator during Steps 1, 2, and 3. No order or directive to coordinate can achieve coordination.

The second principle is based on the importance of achieving coordination in the early stages of planning the project—Steps 1, 2, and 3. It is clear that after the project plan is approved, reconciling differences that arise from the functional organizations becomes more difficult. The reason the methodology recommends that functional department managers sign off on the charter and the project plan is to ensure that all are in agreement on the goals of the project and to clarify how they are to be attained and where each organization fits into the scheme.

The third principle states that all stakeholders in a project are reciprocally related. When A works with B, for example, each finds himself influenced by the other, and both are influenced by all persons in the total situation.

These principles indicate, finally, that the method of achieving coordination is largely horizontal rather than vertical. People cooperate as a result of understanding one another's activities and as a result of participating in the project's planning.

Communications management is simply an ongoing effort by the project manager to ensure coordination of work effort by keeping the team members informed and participating in the project management process and methodology.

PROJECT PROCUREMENT MANAGEMENT

Project procurement management is a facilitating element that deals with acquiring goods and services from outside the immediate project organization; the project manager is the buyer or customer. Of course, the project may have been established as the result of a procurement process (Scenario 4); in that event, the project manager also is also a seller (Scenario 5).

The goal and definition of project procurement management is to develop and implement a formal agreement to procure products or services so that both the buyer and the seller are satisfied with the outcome.

Most organizations have formal, well-defined procurement processes. These documented processes must be followed carefully so that the validity of the resulting contracts is not challenged and so that the procurement process is fair to qualified bidders. The project manager must be aware that the procurement process, especially where competitive bids are required, can be lengthy. It is important to keep this lead time in mind when committing to a schedule that includes subcontracted work or items.

Figure 4.8 illustrates the procurement process.

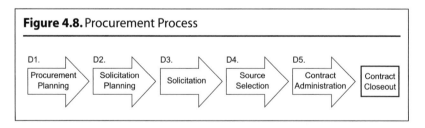

Figure 4.8. Procurement Process

D1. Procurement Planning → D2. Solicitation Planning → D3. Solicitation → D4. Source Selection → D5. Contract Administration → Contract Closeout

D.1 *Procurement Planning*—involves identifying which project needs can best be met by procuring products or services outside the performing organization.

D.2 *Solicitation Planning*—involves preparing the documents needed to support the solicitation process. These include the bid documents provided to the prospective contractors and the evaluation criteria to be used for the selection. The SOW, schedule, and specification are described in the methodology implementing Scenario 3.

D.3 *Solicitation*—involves the development and submission of the bids and proposals by the prospective contractors and the response to questions.

D.4 *Source Selection*—involves receiving bids or proposals and applying the evaluation criteria to select a contractor. Included in this activity is negotiating and establishing a contract.

D.5 *Contract Administration*—involves ensuring that the contractor's and the buyer's performance meets all contractual requirements. Both organizations perform contract administration functions. Contract administration includes ensuring the existence of quality control processes to inspect and verify the adequacy of the contractor's product and change control over scope that affects the formal contract terms.

Many organizations depend on government contracts for their business. All U.S. government agencies use the same basic format for their procurement document for project-type work—the RFP. (Different formats are used when purchasing commodities for which a "request for quotations" is issued.) The same basic elements are found in RFPs issued for projects by private sector and other public sector organizations, including foreign organizations. The reason is simple: These are the elements needed to bid on a project and then include in the subsequent contract. Figure 4.9 contains an annotated table of contents for this format.

Figure 4.9. Solicitation and Contract Sections

NOTES	CONTRACT SECTION AND TITLE	NOTES
A table that contains a list of items/services to be delivered and price for each	A. Solicitation/contract form	Standard form cover page that is used for a signature for submitting a proposal and signing when the contract is awarded
	B. Supplies or services and prices/costs	
Information on how deliverables are to be packaged and identified	C. Description/specifications and/or work statement	Objectives, scope, SOW, requirements, and reference documents
	D. Packaging and marking	
Schedule of when and where each end item is delivered, including quantity	E. Inspection and acceptance	How and where the deliverable items are inspected and accepted; shipping instructions
	F. Deliveries or performance	
	G. Contract administration data	Billing and correspondence instructions, progress payments, names of contacts, authority info, change procedures
Security info, geographic location, unique requirements	H. Special contract requirements	Clauses required by procurement regulations or laws, which pertain to this procurement (boilerplate)
	I. Contract clauses	
A list of items attached to the RFP needed for bidding or as part of the contract	J. List of attachments	
	K. Representations, certifications, and other statements of offerors	Offeror's type of business, cost accounting standards, data rights, tax identification data, etc. (more boilerplate)
Information on how to prepare the proposal, number of copies, format, submittal info	L. Instructions, conditions, and notices to offerors	
	M. Evaluation factors for award	How proposal will be evaluated and what will be evaluated
Specifications, acceptance criteria, statements of work, drawings, technical data packages, etc.	Contract attachments	
	Contract exhibits	Contract data requirements list; data item descriptions, etc.

It is common for RFPs from foreign countries to be identical in format and content to the standard U.S. government template and to reference government documents and specifications.

Figure 4.9 helps put Scenarios 3 and 4 in context, illustrating the various components of an RFP. It is important for new project managers especially to understand the language. It is easy to see how each individual item is necessary, but in total the number of pages can be daunting.

CONFIGURATION MANAGEMENT

"Configuration management" is the process for managing change and knowing where you are in the process for each proposed change. The process has two components: (1) managing any proposed changes to the technical configuration of items being developed and whose performance requirements or design requirements are specified, and (2) managing the scope of the project. The two aspects normally interact because managing technical change usually involves managing changes to contract documents, including budgets and schedules. The feedback loop shown on Figure 1.2 of the basic project management process is often initiated by the need to replan to accommodate technical changes.

The most difficult aspect of configuration management is getting a grasp of the jargon. The principles are very easy.

Configuration management is a discipline that must be implemented at the time of contract award or sometimes before, during proposal preparation and including the project plan. The process of configuration management involves four key subprocesses:

- *Identification*—defining the baseline configuration for the configuration items, providing the basis for control

- *Change control*—controlling the changes to that baseline; reviewing, rejecting, or approving changes and the related documents

- *Status accounting*—accounting for all approved changes; keeping track of each change and the documents and hardware, software, or firmware affected

- *Auditing*—making sure the process is working (e.g., including comparing drawings and specifications to deliverable items to make sure they match).

Some aerospace companies train their new engineers by having them make the approved changes to the affected drawings, thereby learning the drafting system process as well as other internal systems.

In establishing the process used for configuration management on a project, the project manager must designate which deliverables are subject to formal configuration management controls. When working to a contract, usually all deliverables are controlled. A contract deliverable designated for configuration management is called a configuration item. For software, this item is commonly called a computer software configuration item (CSCI).

In addition to deliverables, the contract SOW and WBS become subject to configuration management to control proposed changes that affect them. The WBS and WBS dictionary, scope statement, and statements of work are the documents that define the scope of the project. When the WBS is defined and the project team and customer or sponsor agrees that it is complete, it becomes part of the total baseline for the project. Work not covered by the WBS is not part of the project.

To add or subtract work to the project is to change scope. The project should use a formal process of change management to modify the WBS and supporting documents by adding or deleting work in the SOW and changing project schedules and budgets accordingly. The WBS then becomes a major tool for controlling the phenomenon known as "scope creep." Scope creep arises from unfunded, informal additions to the project work. Abramovici advises: "Controlling scope creep is one of the project manager's major tasks, and he or she has to start working on it even before the project statement of work is written."[18]

When a request for a change is received, either formally or informally, a first step in the analysis is to determine whether or not the change affects the scope of the project. If the work to be performed is covered by the WBS and described in the WBS dictionary or the SOW, then it is in scope. Otherwise, the work is out of scope. In that event, the project manager needs to formally evaluate the impact of the change on cost, schedule, and technical performance, and make the necessary changes to contractual documents and plans to implement the change, if approved.

Configuration management—change control—is not complex, but it is difficult and challenging because there is a strong temptation not to pay attention to the details necessary to document change or formally replan. It is tedious and boring, and it takes effort and discipline—two traits that are often missing in projects.

REFERENCES

1. Gregory T. Haugan. *Project Planning and Scheduling* (Vienna, VA: Management Concepts, Inc., 2002), pp. 88–90.
2. Parviz F. Rad and Ginger Levin. *The Advanced Project Management Office* (Boca Raton, FL: St. Lucie Press, 2002), p. 108.
3. See Robert J. Graham and Randall L. Englund, *Creating an Environment for Successful Projects* (San Francisco: Jossey-Bass Publishers, 1997), for a comprehensive treatment of this topic.
4. See Steven W. Flannes and Ginger Levin, *People Skills for Project Managers* (Vienna, VA: Management Concepts, Inc., 2001) for a current reference on this dimension.
5. Henry Gantt. *Industrial Leadership* (Easton, NY: Hive Publishing Company, 1974), reprint of the 1921 edition published by Associated Press, New York, in series: Page Lecture Series, 1915, Yale University.
6. Peter Drucker. *Management: Tasks, Responsibilities, Practices* (New York: Harper & Row, 1974), p. 402.
7. Harold Koontz and Cyril O'Donnell. *Principles of Management,* 2d ed. (New York: McGraw-Hill, 1959).
8. For an extensive discussion of virtual teams, see Parviz F. Rad and Ginger Levin, *Achieving Project Management Success Using Virtual Teams* (Boca Raton, FL: J. Ross Publishing, Inc., 2003).
9. W. Edwards Deming. *Out of the Crisis* (Cambridge, MA: MIT Center for Advanced Engineering, 1986).
10. *A Guide to the Project Management Body of Knowledge (PMBOK® Guide),* Third Edition (Newtown Square, PA: Project Management Institute, 2004).
11. Paul S. Royer. *Project Risk Management: A Proactive Approach* (Vienna, VA: Management Concepts, Inc., 2002).
12. On December 2, 2003, U.S. Secretary of Defense Donald Rumsfeld won the United Kingdom's Plain English Campaign's annual "Foot in Mouth" award for the most baffling statement by a public figure. Mr. Rumsfeld said in a press briefing, "Reports that say that something hasn't happened are always interesting to me, because as we know, there are known knowns; there are things we know we know. We also know there are known unknowns; that is to say we know there are some things we do not know. But there are also unknown unknowns—the ones we don't know we don't know."
13. See the http://acc.dau.mil website and bibliography for more sophisticated risk models and further discussions of risk management.
14. See also "Team-Based Risk Assessment" by Paula Martin and Karen Tate, *PMI Network,* February 1998, p. 35.
15. Steven W. Flannes and Ginger Levin. *People Skills for Project Managers* (Vienna, VA: Management Concepts, Inc., 2001), p.3.

16. For further discussion, see Harold Koontz and Cyril O'Donnell, *Principles of Management,* 2d ed. (New York: McGraw-Hill, 1959), p. 38.
17. H.C. Metcalf, and L. Urwick, eds. *Dynamic Administration: The Collected Papers of Mary Parker Follett* (New York: Harper & Brothers, 1941), p. 297.
18. Adrian Abramovici. "Controlling Scope Creep." *PMNetwork,* January 2000, pp. 44–48.

Project Management Maturity Models

Projects today are increasingly an asset and a major component of almost every organization's work. As a result, project management tools and techniques are being applied to some extent in almost every company worldwide. Effective project management now is considered an essential value proposition for organizations to improve their competitive edge and to ensure that they remain leaders in their fields.

Organizations with a progressive standard to foster project management improvement evaluate then conduct a project management maturity assessment using a project management maturity model, to evaluate where they can improve in implementing good project management practices. This appendix presents a brief overview of project management maturity and the importance of conducting a maturity assessment.

THE IMPORTANCE OF PROJECT MANAGEMENT MATURITY

Maturity, according to the *Webster's New World Dictionary*, is defined as being full-grown or fully developed. As used here, it also connotes understanding of why success occurs and ways to prevent common problems. This leads to repeatable success in applying project management principles. It also is noteworthy that all organizations go through a maturity

---

Much of the material in this appendix is derived from a paper written by Dr. Parviz Rad and Dr. Ginger Levin titled "Achieving Excellence in Project Management – Project Management Maturity" and is used with permission.

process, and this maturity process precedes overall organizational excellence. The learning curve for maturity is measured in years, and once a high level of maturity is reached, the focus then shifts to continuous improvement and sustaining a competitive advantage.

Early models developed for assessing project management maturity followed the approach used by the Software Engineering Institute in its Capability Maturity Model for Software, which used a 1–5 staged scale.[1] These approaches enabled organizational ratings in software development to be compared across industries and even between models. Comparable models have been developed for project management maturity. Figure A.1 presents such a generic maturity model.

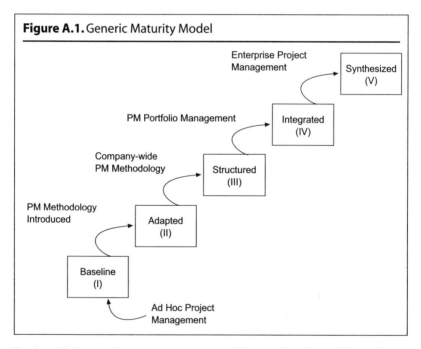

Figure A.1. Generic Maturity Model

In Level 1, project management, if practiced at all, is done in an ad-hoc manner throughout the organization. No standard processes and procedures are performed; standard tools and techniques are not used. Planning consists of only a

Gantt chart schedule, although occasionally individual project managers may be using MS Project® or some other basic project management software.

In Level 2, project management practices are being introduced in the organization, and an organization project management methodology is being prepared and implemented. Project charters and work breakdown structures are prepared. Project plans are prepared, approved, and issued, and a schedule baseline is established

This book addresses all the items necessary for an organization to achieve at least Level II status.

In Level 3, project management is accepted and used throughout the organization and is documented in a company-wide methodology. A group is established as the focal point for project management methodology development and deployment. Documented procedures for time management are part of the organization's standard project management methodology. Resource planning and resource leveling are performed in conjunction with activity network planning. Earned value techniques are used on selected projects. Schedule performance is monitored as part of a schedule control system, and changes are formally administered.

In Level 4, project management is viewed in the organization as supportive and necessary to achieve business goals. A "management by projects" philosophy is followed. Portfolio management is performed to analyze and set priorities for projects. Earned value and other advanced techniques are used for time management including, in some cases, critical chain project management techniques. Planning and scheduling software is standardized, and schedule development and status reporting is performed using a local or wide area network across the company.

In Level 5, project management practices are being continuously improved through a formal process, and project management activities are integrated into an enterprise project management system. The emphasis is on organizational and individual learning to increase project management effectiveness.

A maturity model can be used to determine the existence of realistic and effective project management policies, processes, and procedures. It also is necessary to determine how often and how regularly project personnel follow the established procedures. An established ranking scale in a maturity model will provide plateaus for the purpose of continuous improvement of project management capabilities. The plateau level indicators of the model highlight elements of a specific facet of project management in the organization for identifying key practices that need improvement to elevate the organization's ranking in the specific facet of project management.

An added advantage of evaluating organizational capabilities using a standardized scale through a maturity model is that one can calculate indicators for industry-wide comparisons. These provide a point of pride if the organization ranks favorably, and the motivation to improve if the organization ranks not so favorably.

Higher levels of maturity signify more effective project procedures, higher-quality deliverables, lower project costs, higher project team morale, a desirable balance between cost-schedule-performance (quality), higher levels of customer satisfaction, and ultimately improved profits for the private sector organization. The mature organization is the one that can effectively manage processes. In such an organization, there is an objective, quantitative basis for judging quality and for analyzing problems. As such, expected results for cost, schedule, and functionality are achieved. Further roles and responsibilities are clearly defined, and customer satisfaction is expected as the norm.

Benefits of using a project management maturity model include the ability to assess an organization's current project management capabilities and the ability to identify organizational strengths and weaknesses in project management. Further, the observations made with the use of a maturity model will provide the impetus to establish uniform project management practices within the enterprise, to provide capabilities for transferring knowledge from one project's experience into the next project, and to formulate continuous improvement methodologies for project management procedures.

The benefits of adopting and using evaluation models extend into the details of project performance by fostering improved performance in the areas of cost, schedule, scope, and quality. The results of evaluation models further establish a baseline for improvement objectives if the organization chooses to become project oriented with predictable project success rates. The focus of the assessment is to provide the foundation for improvement and guidance for advancement.

THE ORGANIZATIONAL PROJECT MANAGEMENT MATURITY MODEL

In the same fashion that project evaluation models measure the sophistication of the project team in carrying out the missions of a single project, an organizational project management maturity model (OPM3) measures the ability of the collective organizational project management staff to deliver projects meeting specifications on time and within budget.

In December 2003, after eight years of effort, the Project Management Institute (PMI) published its standard, *Organizational Project Management Maturity Model (OPM3).*[2] This organizational model evolved from the generic model illustrated in Figure A.1.

PMI states: "OPM3 is designed to help organizations translate strategy into successful outcomes, consistently and predictably" (page ix). It is focused on ways in which the organization can reexamine its pursuit of strategic objectives through best practices in organizational project management. It is based on the idea that there is a correlation between project management, program management, and portfolio management and the effectiveness in influencing organizational strategy.

OPM3 is comprised of three general elements: knowledge, which presents the contents of the OPM3 standard; assessment, which provides a method for comparison with the standard; and improvement, which sets the stage for possible organizational changes. OPM3 provides a body of knowledge on the subject of organizational project management. It contains an assessment tool to determine strengths and weaknesses in relation to the best practices in the model with a self-assessment tool that helps assess capabilities in one or more of the best practices that need attention. The results of the assessment then present a list of capabilities that are not fully developed in the organization in a prioritized order of importance to form the basis for future plans for continuous project management improvement.

Its intent is to be prescriptive and enable the organization to make its own informed decisions regarding potential initiatives for change. Therefore, it offers the following benefits to organizations, as summarized from the standard (pages ix and x):

- Strengthen the link between strategic planning and execution. This is important to ensure that project outcomes are predictable, reliable, and consistent and also correlate with organizational success.

- Identify the specific best practices to support the implementation of organizational strategy through successful projects.

- Identify the specific capabilities that make up the best practices and their dependencies.

- Describe these capabilities and best practices in terms of projects, programs, and portfolios.

- Provide a way to assess an organization's maturity.

- Provide a basis from which organizations can make improvements in maturity.

CONDUCTING A PROJECT MANAGEMENT MATURITY ASSESSMENT

The project management maturity assessment is the foundation for continuous improvement in project management practices. There are a number of steps to follow in conducting an assessment. First, note that the assessment is something that the organization decides to do; it is not like an audit, which often is imposed externally. The organization is using the assessment as a way to highlight overall improvements that need to be made. It also is important to define the scope of the assessment—will it be applied to the entire organization, a sector, a business unit, a department, etc.? The people who will be involved in the assessment and the project artifacts to be examined also need to be identified. The people particularly need to prepare for the activity.

A kickoff meeting explains the purpose of the assessment, demonstrates executive support for it, and describes roles, responsibilities, and the schedule. This kickoff meeting also details how the results from the assessment are to be used throughout the organization.

Then, data are collected, analyzed, and verified with the people in the organization who are sponsoring the assessment. The sources for the data are project managers, program managers, portfolio mangers, project team members, functional managers, customers, and the staff in the project management office (if one exists). Survey instruments include questionnaires, interviews, and reviews of organizational and project-specific documents.

After the data are analyzed, an organizational ranking is prepared along with a report summarizing the assessment process and, more importantly, presenting a plan of prioritized improvement actions. The recommendations generated highlight improvement in the project management knowledge areas and in terms of projects, programs, and portfolios. The assessment report provides a guidebook that describes which improvements should be undertaken first. Because the improvements are tied to the assessment itself, assessment findings help communicate the need for changes to the rest of the organization, promote a commitment for the improvement initiatives, and heighten project management visibility.

SUMMARY

Project management organizational maturity models measure the ability and likelihood of the collective organizational project management staff to deliver projects on time, according to specifications, and within budget. Higher levels of maturity signify more effective project procedures, higher-quality deliverables, lower project costs, higher levels of customer satisfaction, and improved organizational profits. Lower levels of maturity, on the other hand, show an organization that probably has repeated experience with failed projects, that implements redundant and conflicting procedures, and that has a history of misdirected improvement initiatives.

REFERENCES

1. CMU/SEI Technical Report 24-93, Capability Maturity Model for Software, Version 1.1 (Pittsburgh, PA: Software Engineering Institute, Carnegie Mellon University, February 1993).

2. Project Management Institute. *Organizational Project Management Maturity Model (OPM3)* (Newtown Square, PA: Project Management Institute, 2003).

Advanced Project Management Concepts for Further Study

This book covers the basic methodology needed to manage a project. However, project managers should be aware of some additional project management techniques and concepts. A brief description of each follows, and additional references can be found in the bibliography.

EARNED VALUE MANAGEMENT SYSTEM

A widely used technique for managing projects in the Department of Defense, NASA, and the Department of Energy for more than 35 years is known as "earned value." The Office of Management and Budget (OMB) currently requires that this methodology be used on all large government procurements.[1]

Earned value is an industry acceptable cost/schedule tool that permits the project manager, or usually the project scheduler, to quantify the work performed in terms of "earned hours" and then to compare this number with both planned and expended hours for any given status date. It thus compares the amount of work that was planned with what actually has been accomplished to determine if progress is as planned. The conclusions that can be derived from these comparisons allow the scheduler to isolate both resource overruns or underruns as well as to forecast the estimate at completion for the project, or WBS element.

Five terms are generally used in the current concept of earned value:

1. BCWS—Budgeted costs for work scheduled is the plan against which performance will be measured. It is the cumulative planned cost curve.

2. BCWP/(EV)—Budgeted costs for work performed is the earned value or dollar value of the work accomplished against the plan. It is the cumulative value of the work completed, using the budgeted data.

3. ACWP—Actual costs of work performed are the actual costs incurred as reported by the accounting system, or the cumulative actual cost curve.

4. BAC—Budget at completion is the projected value of the plan (BCWS) at the end of the project.

5. EAC—Estimate at completion is the projected value of what the effort will actually cost (ACWP) at the end of the project.

The unique concept is the BCWP or earned value derived from the data used to develop the top-level expenditure plan, the BCWS. This is developed as a three-step process and represents the cumulative value of the work packages or cost accounts of the project that have been completed. As the project proceeds and each work package is completed, the value of that work package, as indicated by the original budgeted amount (not the actual expenditure), is tabulated as "earned." This cumulative tabulation, when spread by time, is the BCWP/EV. Credit is taken for work completed only at the budgeted or planned level. Many different types of analyses and displays of data are possible using these data.

One of the many references to earned value should be consulted if you are assigned to a large project. While the concept is simple, the implementation is not.

Most current project management software programs have the capability to provide earned value calculations and output. To implement EVMS, certain criteria must be met during the planning phase, and the chart of accounts and the accounting system must have certain capabilities.

The industry standard describing the EVMS is EIA-748-A, Earned Value Management Systems, published in January 2002 by the Electronic Industries Alliance of Arlington, Virginia, in accordance with ANSI standards. Other useful EVMS reference documents are available on the Internet:

- Department of Defense earned value implementation manual (EVIM): http://guidebook.dcma.mil/79/evmi-goldversion.doc

- Department of Energy's guide for EVM: http://www.oecm.energy.gov/Portals/2/DOEEVMApplicationGuide-March252005.doc

- Department of Energy's tutorial for EVM: http://www.oecm.energy.gov/Default.aspx?tabid=142 - (breaks EVMS down into modules/step-by-step guide

- NASA's website for EVMS: http://evm.nasa.gov/index.html.

CRITICAL CHAIN PROJECT MANAGEMENT

In 1984, Dr. Eliyahu M. Goldratt wrote a book titled *The Goal*. This book, which addresses production and inventory problems in the factory, presented and explained his "Theory of Constraints." In 1997, he followed up with a similar book titled *Critical Chain*, which addressed the project management process. His methodology and philosophy are receiving increasing attention as more and more organizations are implementing it successfully.

Critical chain project management (CCPM) varies from the methodology in this book and the management literature in six areas. To understand them completely, and to implement them successfully, it may be necessary to read *Critical Chain* and other CCPM books because of the level of detail and understanding of scheduling required.[2] The six areas are as follows:

1. CCPM specifies the "critical chain" and not the logic network "critical path" as the primary project constraint. The critical chain (CC) considers resource dependencies as well as activity dependencies and tends to remain unchanged during project implementation.

2. CCPM uses 50 percent probable activity duration estimates, not the normal 90 percent or low-risk padded estimates in common use. Activity contingency is not permitted.

3. To allow for the uncertainty of the estimates and the eventual variations in actual performance, allowances are aggregated into "buffers" at the end of activity chains. Buffers also are provided for resources. The buffers represent the project contingency.

4. The size of the buffers is used as the primary measurement tool or metric for schedule control.

5. When multiple projects are being performed within an organization and there is resource sharing, the constraining "company resource" is identified. This resource becomes the focal point or axis for scheduling all projects.

6. CCPM requires changes in project team and management behavior, encouraging early completion and reporting of activities, no sanctions for exceeding expected durations (within some rules), and elimination or significant reduction in multitasking.

The development of a critical chain plan involves a series of standard steps:

- Develop a "normal" logic network-based plan, including customary estimating of activity durations (including padding as usual).

- Modify the network-based plan to eliminate all resource constraints (use leveling or a variation thereof). Where necessary, extend the start of activities where there is a resource constraint.

- Re-estimate activity durations at the 50 percent probability level, and use the difference between the two estimates to size the buffers, "Δt."

- Insert a "project buffer" at the end of the project (several formulas for the size of the buffer are used; one is to use one-half of the sum of the Δts from the critical chain path).

- Insert a "feeding path" buffer at the end of each path that feeds the critical chain. (Use the same formula as above for the size of the buffer).

- Establish a resource buffer for resources required to support the critical chain. (These may be in the form of alerts and do not add time to the critical chain.)

- For noncritical chain paths, delay the start to the "latest start" date.

- Focus on the completion of the project and not on individual activities. Make sure each resource starts work as soon as input is received, works 100 percent on the activity (no multitasking), and passes on the work as soon as it is finished.

- There is no penalty for completing activities later than the estimated duration; after all, at 50 percent probability, approximately half should finish later. "No penalty" assumes starting as soon as possible if on the critical chain and working 100 percent of the time on the activity, with no multitasking.

Schedule control is exercised by monitoring the impact of activity completion on the size of the buffers. Frequent solicitations of estimates-to-complete are made. Corrective action is initiated only when a significant percentage (approximately 50 percent) of the buffer is used.

It is claimed that all projects that "have diligently applied CCPM have completed the project substantially under the original time, fulfilled the original scope, and came in near or under the original budget."[3]

REFERENCES

1. For the application on government programs, see Gregory T. Haugan, *The Work Breakdown Structure in Government Contracting* (Vienna, VA: Management Concepts, Inc., 2003).
2. Lawrence P. Leach. *Critical Chain Project Management* (Boston, MA: Artech House, Inc., 2000).
3. Ibid.

Project Life Cycles

The concept of life cycle is easy to understand. But like many concepts in project management, applying the term is confusing because it applies to several types of items. The two major types of life cycles are product (or program) and project life cycles.

The product life cycle identifies the phases of the product from the time the original concept was conceived through development, being put into service by the customer, and finally destroyed or salvaged. Product life-cycle cost analysis includes estimating and comparing the total costs of two or more approaches to achieving the same objectives, considering the maintenance costs of the product over its service life as well as development and production costs.

Part 5 of this book discusses project versus program (or product) management as relates to life cycles. This appendix, however, discusses project life cycles because this book focuses on project management more than on program or product management.

Projects have a beginning, a specified duration, and an end; they start, work continues, and then they finish. The project is finished, and the deliverable item or end item is turned over to the customer to use or to put into operation. The separate generic phases are often referred to as initiation, planning, execution, and closeout. Certain work is performed in each phase, and each phase may be independently planned and managed within the overall project life cycle.

It is important to recognize where a project fits within its overall life cycle because it affects the application of the methodology. Part 3 of this book discusses seven scenarios and how the application of the methodology varies depending on the life-cycle phase.

Note that we are discussing the project life cycle (see Figure C.1), and not the life cycle of the product or the program.

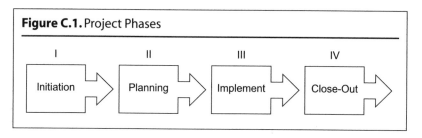

Figure C.1. Project Phases

When the different phases are addressed explicitly, the generic life-cycle phases of a project are defined as follows:

Initiation Phase—Sometimes called the feasibility or conceptual phase. The phase usually begins with an idea or problem to be solved. During this phase, alternatives are evaluated and selected using a standard problem-solving methodology, economic or quantitative analysis. On smaller projects, the initiation phase may be minimal—a project created during a meeting or by a customer or supervisor to solve a problem. Minimal analysis is performed, often just a simple benefit-cost analysis as part of the project justification. Frequently, project managers are given projects to plan and implement where the initiation phase has been performed by others. When you are bidding on a contract or have been awarded a contract, the initiation phase and usually part of the planning phase have been performed by the customer.

Planning Phase—Sometimes called the development phase or the design phase, the end item is a project plan or a set of drawings. Schedules, budgets, work statements, and specifications are developed and approved for the next phase—the implementation phase. Resources are identified and scheduled. Baselines are established. If the project is to be outsourced, the planning phase is partially completed, and the contractor or organization performing the implementation phase will complete the planning, either in the proposal phase or shortly after contract award.

In one scenario, when an organization is awarded a contract, the planning phase is usually completed the first week or two, during which the detail plans prepared at the time of proposal being submitted are updated and reviewed with the customer. In parallel, long lead-time procurement of material items and certain key activities are initiated. (See Scenario 5 in Part 3.) The completion of the planning phase is characterized by the approval of the project plan or a successful kickoff meeting.

Implementation Phase—The project work is performed and managed according to the plans and schedules developed in the planning phase. Progress is controlled and monitored, and corrective action is taken as necessary. Also, replanning to various degrees occurs in most projects as problems or opportunities arise.

Closeout Phase—A small but important phase is necessary to finish the project. The unique activities necessary to complete the project are performed.

Figure C.2 illustrates the life cycle in terms of the relative amount of resources generally expended in each phase.

Each of these phases has specific output items or milestones that define the beginning and end of the phase—just like a project. While these vary from company to company and

Figure C.2. Project Phase Work Effort

PHASE I INITIATION	PHASE II PLANNING	PHASE III IMPLEMENTATION	PHASE IV CLOSE-OUT
		Area Under Bars Is Rough Approximation of Relative Work Effort	

industry to industry, the generic items that usually are developed in each phase are illustrated in Figure C.3. The outputs from each phase are important to the phase and understanding of the significance of the life-cycle concept as relates to the methodology presented in Part 2.

Figure C.3. Typical Output from Each Project Phase

Phase	Output
INITIATION	Goals and objectives, preliminary planning information, preliminary statement of work, economic analyses, preliminary cost estimate, preliminary project charter, business case, solicitation materials, decision memoranda, management decision
PLANNING	Project charter, scope statement, statement of work, work breakdown structure, cost estimate, budget, schedule, project plan, solicitation package
IMPLEMENTATION	Project products, services, results, deliverables, CLINs, CDRLs, plans for operation and maintenance after delivery
CLOSEOUT	Complete all financial, administrative, contractual, and personnel activities, document lessons learned, archive project records

CLIN: Contract Line Item Number (the jargon used in many government contracts to identify the deliverable hardware items and services).
CDRL: Contract Data Requirements List (the jargon used in many government contracts to identify the deliverable data items).

Other life-cycle phase descriptors are used in different industries. For example, the following were identified as typical life cycles in their respective industries:

- Construction project—feasibility, design, bid and award, build, commission, and operate and maintain

- Government acquisition—concept and technology development, system development and demonstration, product and deployment, operation and support, and disposal.

Appendix D contains more detail on the unique life cycle of a typical information technology project.

Many projects (programs) have another phase in the overall life cycle of the product (or result) that is not part of the project but is the responsibility of the customer. It represents what happens after the project is completed and the product delivered. Depending on the product it typically is an operation and maintenance phase; it is referred to as a warranty period or postdeployment support for IT projects. During the initiation phase and often as part of a solicitation, life-cycle costs are calculated. These include the operational and maintenance costs of the product until the end of its useful life.

One of the main purposes of the initiation phase is to clarify the vision/strategy/mission/purpose of the project and, as part of establishing the business case for the project, convert general statements into quantifiable performance measurements. These metrics are used to monitor progress and, when appropriate, to terminate the project.

Because the work within each phase can be defined as a project, the basic project management process applies to the work performed within each phase and not just to the combined planning and implementation phase. For example, the work performed in the initiation phase can (and should on larger projects) be planned and managed as a stand-alone project. The initiation phase usually has a target completion date, an approximate budget, and an expected level of performance of the final product, which is frequently used as part of the project justification package.

The planning phase also has specified output products, completion dates, budgets, and performance criteria with this information packaged in a formal project plan document. The output of the planning phase may be a solicitation package if the product is to be procured outside the organization. It varies with the scenario, as demonstrated in Part 3.

In smaller projects, especially in-house projects (Scenario 1), the lines between the phases become blurred, and once a decision is made to proceed, the planning and implementation phase are not as clearly separated, as shown in Figure C.4).

Figure C.4. Life Cycle—Smaller Projects

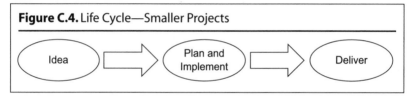

The project manager often is inclined to start the implementation phase as rapidly as possible, without sufficient planning. The planning phase must not be ignored or minimized since this is a recipe for disaster and cost overruns. There must be sufficient planning and a formal review of the planning before jumping into full-scale development or implementation.

The minimum plan on a small project should be a resource-loaded schedule using project management software to identify the activities and responsibilities for each activity. This may take from a few hours to a few days to complete and coordinate with the project team.

Information Technology Program Life Cycle

Information technology programs/projects have their own life cycle and their own language for the work performed. The life cycle is somewhat different from the generic project management life cycle, but the same concept applies: there are discrete phases or stages where work is performed to plan and define the project and an implementation phase to perform the major work and deliver the final products.

Figure D.1 presents the typical output from each IT life-cycle phase.

Figure D.1. Typical Output from Each IT Life-Cycle Phase

Phase/Stage	Output
Concept	Problem or desired change results in a recommendation to initiate a project
Initiation	Overall project plan and a plan for the design phase
Design	Analysis, logical design, physical design
Implementation	Project products, deliverables, plans for operation, and maintenance phase
Closeout	Complete all financial, administrative, contractual, and personnel activities

Note that the definition of "initiation" by custom is different for IT projects from that used in the project management methodology for a generic life cycle.

Material used in this section is adapted from Florida Department of Revenue IT Project Development Template, October 2004.

PROJECT CONCEPT STAGE

All projects are started for a reason: to improve a process or product, or to develop a new process or product, and all start with an idea or a need. This results in action being initiated to start a project. The output of the project concept stage is this idea or need.

PROJECT INITIATION STAGE

At the start of any project, there will be a variety of ideas and opinions about the purpose and scope of the project, what the final product of the project will be, and how the project will be carried out. The project initiation stage is concerned with taking these ideas and intentions and developing them into a formal, planned, resourced, and funded project.

To define a project in this way, it is first necessary to clearly and explicitly define what the project is intended to achieve and what its scope of interest will be. By defining this first, a benchmark is created for assessing the quality of what is actually produced at the end of the project.

The project initiation stage also must define what resources and associated time commitment are required to carry out the project.

Initially, the overall project schedule is not at a sufficient level of detail to enable the allocation of actual resources to activities or to control progress. It is necessary to produce a more detailed plan for these purposes. This detailed plan is produced only for the next stage of the project, usually covering an elapsed time of two to four months.

The way the project is managed and executed is the key to its success. Involving the right people for data capture and decision making also is crucial. It is necessary to identify and recruit these people at the start of the project and to define the project organization structure. It also is necessary to establish the procedures that will be used by the people in the project organization structure to carry out and control the project work.

Finally, to establish a resourced and funded project, it is necessary to establish a clear and convincing business case for the project. This business case should be reviewed and accepted by management. The business case will identify the projected benefits of meeting the objectives of the project and balance these against the costs and risks associated with realizing these benefits. The business case also can be used as a benchmark to compare against actual results, costs, and benefits to assess the ultimate success of the project.

The project initiation stage is performed as a sequence of steps. Many of these steps occur in parallel, and the step products are developed iteratively, because there are many dependencies between the steps. Despite this, project initiation should be conducted in a relatively short timeframe when compared to the rest of the project. Aim for two to four weeks elapsed time.

The product of the project initiation stage is an overall plan for carrying out the whole project and a more detailed plan for the next stage of the project: the design phase. A project schedule often is confused with a project plan. A schedule is one component of a plan. The complete plan for the project consists of:

• Clearly defined scope

• Overall schedule of activities for the project

• Project organization

- Clearly defined project control procedures to:

  - check and confirm quality

  - control resource/cost/time

  - manage change

  - manage issues

- Clearly stated business case for the project

- Budget for the project.

In addition, the plan for the next stage consists of:

- Detailed schedule of activities for the stage

- Quality review standards for products to be produced

- Identified resources and associated costs

- Control tolerances.

DESIGN STAGE

The objective of the design stage is to define and design a new system in a way that: (1) rapidly establishes, agrees on, and prioritizes the critical requirements for the new system; (2) develops a functional description (data and process models) of the required system; (3) establishes a prototype based on real-world business scenarios; (4) establishes a detailed set of acceptance criteria and an associated system test; (5) produces a logical design for the system; and (6) produces a detailed physical design for the system so that its construction can begin more quickly.

The steps and tasks contained in this template represent a subset of:

- Analysis

- Logical design

- Physical design.

IMPLEMENTATION STAGE

The objective of the implementation stage is to build and implement the system in a way that meets the agreed specifications, tests for defects, and implements live running of the system in the production environment so that users can begin live running of the system.

This stage develops and implements the application.

CLOSEOUT STAGE

The closeout stage is the same as the generic project management methodology. All loose ends are tied up, and the project is completed.

Types of Projects

The recently assigned project manager must be aware that there are different types of projects and that each is approached somewhat differently in the application of the steps of the methodology. Four types of projects are:

1. *Product*—the deliverable is a specific, well-defined product with specified performance

2. *Service*—the deliverable is a service that is defined and provided

3. *Result*—the end product is a result that occurs at the end of the project

4. *Structured result*—an end product that is achieved by following a structured methodology in addition to the project management methodology.

The differences between these four types of projects are important to the application of certain steps of the methodology.

PRODUCT-BASED PROJECT

In a product-based project the deliverable is a specific, well-defined physical product with a clearly specified or communicated performance. These types of projects have a tangible output product (a building, dam, airplane, bicycle, tank, sewer system, and road intersection are possible big projects, and an instruction manual, marketing brochure, and dog house are possible smaller projects). These products all have a defined structure.

Large projects typically have a design, development, fabrication, component test, and system test set of work packages for each major subassembly and detail part. Smaller projects may include graphics, preliminary draft, story board, and reports just for the end item.

SERVICE-BASED PROJECT

Service projects do not have a tangible, structured deliverable; the output is a defined body of work accomplished for a customer. Typical projects in this category include putting on a conference, having a party or a wedding, planning a vacation trip, and moving an office to a new location. In all of these projects, the deliverable is a successful event measured in terms of all the separate activities being performed in accordance with a time table and meeting a specified date within a specified budget. Performance is measured in terms of the event "coming off without a hitch."

RESULTS-BASED PROJECT

Results projects do not have a tangible, structured deliverable. The output is the result of a process or subprojects that "result" in a product or a conclusion (e.g. cancer research, new drug development, culture change). The project involves performing a series of planned steps leading to a result that occurs at a specific planned point in time and within a budget. This is typical of research projects.

For example, the project may be to implement a new process in a factory where the process performs in accordance with a specification. Many pharmaceutical development projects fall into this category.

STRUCTURED PRODUCT

The structure project proceeds based on a combination of project management principles and a formal structured methodology such as is used for IT software development. The project follows a series of specified steps to the eventual delivery of the tested product. If there is no specified methodology, the project would probably fall into the "product" or "result" category. Appendix D contains a description of an IT development process life cycle.

Bibliography

Anthony, Robert N. *Planning and Control Systems: A Framework for Analysis.* Boston: Graduate School of Business Administration, Harvard University, 1965.

Arizona State University. "Question List for Software Risk Identification in the Classroom." www.ieas.asu.edu/ ~riskmgmt/qlist.html.

Associated General Contractors. *CPM in Construction: A Manual for General Contractors.* Washington, D.C.: Associated General Contractors, 1965.

Carroll, Lewis. *The Complete Works of Lewis Carroll.* New York: The Modern Library, Random House, 1922.

Cioffi, Denis F. *Managing Project Integration.* Vienna, VA: Management Concepts, Inc., 2002.

Clark, C. "The Optimum Allocation of Resources Among Activities of a Network." *Journal of Industrial Engineering,* vol. 12 (January-February, 1961): 11–17.

Cleland, David I., and Lewis R. Ireland. *Project Manager's Portable Handbook.* 2d ed. New York: McGraw Hill, 2004.

Cole, Peter S. *How to Write a Statement of Work.* 5th ed. Vienna, VA: Management Concepts, Inc., 2003.

Dale, Ernest. *Management: Theory and Practice.* New York: Mc-Graw-Hill, 1965.

Deming, W. Edward. *Out of the Crisis.* Cambridge, MA: Massachusetts Institute of Technology Center for Advanced Engineering Study, 1985.

Dobson, Michael S. *The Triple Constraints in Project Management.* Vienna, VA: Management Concepts, Inc., 2004.

Drucker, Peter F. *Management: Tasks, Responsibilities, Practices.* New York: Harper & Row, 1974.

Engelbeck, Marshall R. *Acquisition Management.* Vienna, VA: Management Concepts, Inc., 2002.

Flannes, Steven W., and Ginger Levin. *People Skills for Project Managers:* Vienna, VA: Management Concepts, Inc., 2001.

Fleming, Quentin W. *Put Earned Value (C/SCSC) Into Your Management Control System.* Worthington, OH: Publishing Horizons, Inc., 1983.

Gantt, Henry L. *Industrial Leadership.* Easton, NY: Hive Publishing Company, 1974. Reprint of 1921 Edition Published by Association Press, New York, in Series: Page Lecture Series, Yale University, 1915.

Gantt, Henry L. *Organizing for Work,* Easton: Hive Publishing Company, 1974, Reprint of 1919 edition published by Harcourt, Brace and Howe, New York.

Gantt, Henry L. *Work Wages, and Profits.* 2d ed. Easton, NY: Hive Publishing Company, 1974.

Goldratt, Eliyahu M. *Critical Chain.* Great Barrington, MA: The North River Press, 1997.

Goldratt, Eliyahu M. *The Goal.* 2d ed. Great Barrington, MA: The North River Press, 1992.

Goodpasture, John C. *Managing Projects for Value.* Vienna, VA: Management Concepts, Inc., 2002.

Goodstein, Leonard, Timothy Nolan, and J. William Pfeiffer. *Applied Strategic Planning: A Comprehensive Guide.* San Diego: Pfeiffer & Co., 1992.

Graham, Robert J., and Randall L. Englund. *Creating an Environment for Successful Projects.* San Francisco: Jossey-Bass Publishers, 1997.

Haugan, Gregory T. *Effective Work Breakdown Structures.* Vienna, VA: Management Concepts, Inc., 2002.

Haugan, Gregory T. *Project Planning and Control.* Vienna, VA: Management Concepts, Inc., 2003.

Haugan, Gregory T. *The Work Breakdown Structure in Government Contracting.* Vienna, VA: Management Concepts, Inc., 2003.

Haugan, Gregory T. *PERT.* Baltimore: Martin Marietta Aerospace Division, 1962.

Haugan, Gregory T. *Primer—Project Management Methodology* Heathsville, VA: GLH, Inc., 1998.

Higuera, Ron, and Yacov Haimes. *Software Risk Management.* Pittsburg, PA: Software Engineering Institute, 1996.

Huston, Charles L. *Management of Project Procurement.* New York: McGraw-Hill, 1996.

Iannone, Anthony L. *Management Program Planning and Control with PERT, MOST and LOB.* Englewood Cliffs, NJ: Prentice-Hall Inc., 1967.

Kelley, J. "Critical Path Planning and Scheduling: Mathematical Basis." *Operations Research,* vol. 9 (May-June, 1961): 296–321.

Kerzner, Harold. *Project Management: A Systems Approach to Planning Scheduling and Controlling.* 7th ed. New York: John Wiley & Sons, 2001.

Kerzner, Harold. *Strategic Planning for Project Management Using a Project Management Maturity Model.* New York: John Wiley & Sons, 2001.

Kloppenborg, Timothy J., and Joseph A. Petrick. *Managing Project Quality.* Vienna, VA: Management Concepts, Inc., 2002.

Koontz, Harold, and Cyril O'Donnell. *Principles of Management.* 2d ed. New York: McGraw-Hill, 1959.

Leach, Lawrence P. *Critical Chain Project Management.* Boston, MA: Artech House, Inc., 2000.

Levin, Ginger, et al. *ProjectFRAMEWORK: A Project Management Maturity Model.* Arlington, VA: ESI International, 1999.

Lock, Dennis, ed. *Project Management Handbook.* Aldershot, England: Gower Technical Press, Ltd., 1987.

Malcolm, D.G., J.H. Roseboom, C.E. Clark, and W. Fazar. "Application of a Technique for Research and Development Program Evaluation." *Operations Research,* vol. 7 (September-October 1959); 646–670.

Martin, Michael G. *Delivering Project Excellence with the Statement of Work.* Vienna, VA: Management Concepts, Inc., 2003.

Martino, R.L. *Finding the Critical Path.* New York: American Management Association, 1964.

Meredith, Jack R., and Samuel J. Mantel, Jr. *Project Management: A Managerial Approach.* 3d ed. New York: John Wiley & Sons, 1995.

Miller, Robert W. *Schedule, Cost and Profit Control with PERT.* New York: McGraw-Hill, 1963.

Neuendorf, Steve. *Six Sigma for Project Managers.* Vienna, VA: Management Concepts, Inc., 2004.

Neuendorf, Steve. *Project Measurement.* Vienna, VA: Management Concepts, Inc., 2002.

Nutt, Howard, Nancy Kessler, and Ginger Levin. *Business Development Capability Maturity Model.* Farmington, UT: Shipley Associates, 2003.

Office of Naval Material. *Line of Balance Technology.* Department of the Navy, NAVEXOS P 1851, 24 February 1958.

Pacelli, Lonnie. *Project Management Advisor: 18 Major Project Screw-ups, and How to Cut Them Off at the Pass.* Upper Saddle River, NJ: Prentice Hall, 2004.

Project Management Institute. *A Guide to the Project Management Body of Knowledge (PMBOK® Guide),* 3d ed. Newton Square, PA: Project Management Institute, 2004.

Project Management Institute. *Organizational Project Management Maturity Model (OPM3) Knowledge Foundation.* Newtown Square, PA: Project Management Institute, 2003.

Rad, Parviz F., and Ginger Levin. *Achieving Project Management Success Using Virtual Teams.* Boca Raton, FL: J. Ross Publishing, 2003.

Rad, Parviz F., and Ginger Levin. *The Advanced Project Management Office.* Boca Raton, FL: St. Lucie Press, 2002.

Rad, Parviz F., and Ginger Levin. *Metrics for Project Management.* Vienna, VA: Management Concepts, 2006.

Rosenau, Milton D., Jr. *Project Management for Engineers.* Belmont, CA: Lifetime Learning Publications, 1984.

Rosenau, Milton D., Jr. *Successful Project Management.* 3d ed. New York: John Wiley & Sons, Inc., 1998.

The System Company. *How Scientific Management Is Applied (A series of 10 essays).* 2d rev. ed. London: A.W. Shaw Company, Ltd., 1911.

U.S. Department of Defense. "Risk Management." *Crosstalk Journal of Defense Software Engineering,* February 2005, www.stsc.hill.af.mil.

U.S. Department of Defense. *Handbook for Preparation of Statement of Work.* MIL-HDBK-245D, 3 April 1996.

U.S. Department of Defense. *Work Breakdown Structures.* MIL-HDBK-881, 2 January 1998.

U.S. Department of Defense. *Defense and Program-Unique Specifications Format and Content.* MIL-STD-961E, 1 August 2003.

U.S. Department of Defense. *Risk Management Guide for DoD Acquisition.* Ft. Belvoir, VA: Defense Acquisition University, June 2003. www.dsmc.dsm.mil/pubs/gdbks/risk_management.htm.

U.S. Department of Energy. *Risk Assessment Questionnaire.* http://cio.doe.gov./sqse/pm_risk.htm.

Index

deliverables and requirements, initiating stage, 18–20
detail specification, initiating stage, 42
direct assignment from another organization scenario
define deliverables and requirements, 156
overview, 141–142, 154
project phase in the life cycle, 155–156
direct assignment from supervisor or sponsor scenario
approve project plan, 154
assign and schedule resources and costs, 151–152
define activities and durations, 150–151
define deliverables and requirements, 148
develop checkpoints and performance measures, 153
develop cost estimate, 152–153
develop logical network and schedule, 150–151
develop project charter, 148
develop project plan, 153–154
develop statement of objectives, 147
develop work breakdown structure, 149
establish project baselines, 153
overview, 141
plan work, 150
prepare specification, 149–150
prepare statement of work, 149
project phase in the life cycle, 146
direct costs, performance tracking, 114, 117

DoD. *See* U.S. Department of Defense

E

early finish (EF), 65
early start (ES), 65
earned value management system (EVMS), 89, 114
EF. *See* early finish
environmental elements
issue procedures and directives, 207–208
management support, 204–206
overview, 203–204
project management software, 207
environmental problems, 199
ES. *See* early start
EVMS. *See* earned value management system
executing stage
methodology, 97
performing work, process overview, 98
project management process, 7
purpose, 96
expeditor, 214

F

facilitating problems, 200
Factory Acceptance Test (FAT), 88
feasibility phase. *See* initiating phase
finish-to-finish (FF) relationship, 62
finish-to-start (FS) relationship, 62
flexibility matrix, 22